DISCARD

ESSENTIAL CHEMISTRY

BIOCHEMISTRY

ESSENTIAL CHEMISTRY

Atoms, Molecules, and Compounds

Chemical Reactions

Metals

The Periodic Table

States of Matter

Acids and Bases

Biochemistry

Carbon Chemistry

Chemical Bonds

Earth Chemistry

ESSENTIAL CHEMISTRY

BIOCHEMISTRY

MONIQUE LABERGE, PH.D.

CHELSEA HOUSE
PUBLISHERS
An imprint of Infobase Publishing

BIOCHEMISTRY

Chelsea House
An imprint of Infobase Publishing
132 West 31st Street
New York NY 10001

Library of Congress Cataloging-in-Publication Data

Laberge, Monique.
  Biochemistry / Monique Laberge.
    p. cm. — (Essential chemistry)
  Includes bibliographical references and index.
  ISBN 978–0-7910–9693–2 (hardcover)
  1. Biochemistry—Textbooks. I. Title. II. Series.

  QP514.2.L33 2008
  612'.015—dc22   2007051316

Chelsea House books are available at special discounts when purchased in bulk quantities for businesses, associations, institutions, or sales promotions. Please call our Special Sales Department in New York at (212) 967–8800 or (800) 322–8755.

You can find Chelsea House on the World Wide Web at http://www.chelseahouse.com

Text design by Erik Lindstrom
Cover design by Ben Peterson
Composition by North Market Street Graphics
Cover printed by Bang Printing, Brainerd, MN
Book printed and bound by Bang Printing, Brainerd, MN
Date printed: January, 2010
Printed in the United States of America

10 9 8 7 6 5 4 3

This book is printed on acid-free paper.

All links and Web addresses were checked and verified to be correct at the time of publication. Because of the dynamic nature of the Web, some addresses and links may have changed since publication and may no longer be valid.

CONTENTS

1   **What Is Biochemistry?**   1

2   **Amino Acids**   9

3   **Proteins and Nucleic Acids**   16

4   **Enzymes**   31

5   **Lipids and Biological Membranes**   40

6   **Carbohydrates: Energy for Living Organisms**   48

7   **Metabolic Pathways: The Roads to Energy**   54

8   **Photosynthesis: The Basis of Life on Earth**   64

9   **The Human Genome Project**   73

Periodic Table of the Elements   82

Electron Configurations   84

Table of Atomic Masses   86

Glossary   88

Bibliography   100

Further Reading   101

Photo Credits   105

Index   106

About the Author   112

What Is Biochemistry?

Biochemistry is the study of the chemistry of life. It seeks to understand the relationship between the structure and function of the **molecules** that make up living organisms. This is no easy task because of the enormous diversity and complexity of life processes. There is a broad overlap between biochemistry and all of the other sciences that study living organisms, from microorganisms to plants, animals, and human beings. Areas as diverse as cell and molecular biology, molecular genetics, physiology, toxicology, drug design, nutrition, forensic science, and environmental science all use biochemistry techniques and methods.

Some biochemists try to explain how the molecules that make up the human body function. They identify the molecules and determine how the molecules are produced, how they interact with each other, and the results of the chemical reactions they undergo.

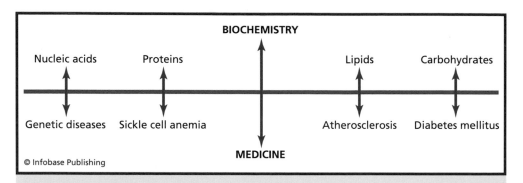

Figure 1.1   **The relationship between biochemistry and medicine is illustrated above. Medical researchers attempt to find cures for the diseases shown in the bottom half of the diagram by investigating the molecules shown in the top half.**

These molecules are mostly found in **cells**, the basic structural units of living systems, or in close proximity to cells.

BIOMOLECULES

Just as there is a great diversity of living organisms, there is also a wide variety of molecules essential to life. These **biomolecules** are usually classified in four major groups: **proteins, nucleic acids, lipids**, and **carbohydrates**. The groups differ in chemical structure, reactivity, and function. Proteins are constructed from compounds called **amino acids**. Some proteins are structural, such as those that make up hair and cartilage; some are reactive, such as the **enzymes** that carry out the numerous chemical reactions of life. **DNA** and **RNA** are nucleic acids, compounds that carry genetic information and control protein **synthesis**. They are among the largest molecules known. Lipids are compounds that include fats and oils. Carbohydrates include such important compounds as **sugars**, starch, and cellulose. Within each of the four main groups of biomolecules are subgroups, classified according to structure or functionality.

Proteins are one of the major constituents of cells. The study of proteins includes two important areas of biochemical specialization, namely protein synthesis and enzymology. Protein synthesis

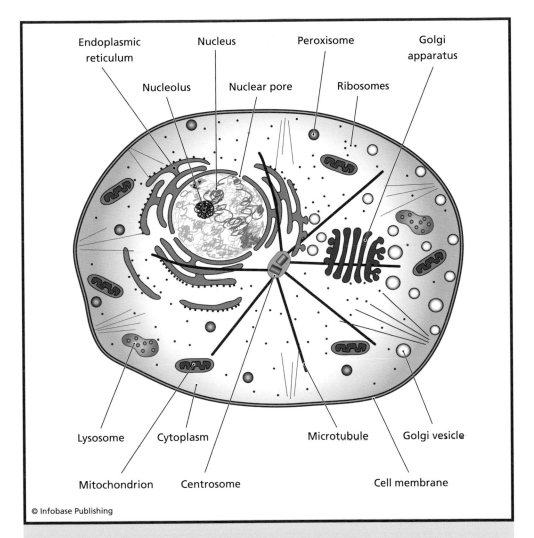

Endoplasmic reticulum

Nucleus

Peroxisome

Golgi apparatus

Nucleolus

Nuclear pore

Ribosomes

Lysosome

Cytoplasm

Microtubule

Golgi vesicle

Mitochondrion

Centrosome

Cell membrane

© Infobase Publishing

Figure 1.2   The cell is the basic unit of life. Above is a diagram of a eukaryote cell, the more complex of the two categories of cells. Unlike the more primitive prokaryotes, eukaryotes have nuclear membranes and membrane-bound organelles.

is the process of how proteins are made. Enzymology is the study of enzymes. Enzymologists describe the sites where enzymes bind and the molecules that can activate or stop them. They also study how enzymes control **metabolism**, the chemical processes occurring within a living cell or organism that are essential for life. Other specialization areas include **cell membrane** transport, the

TABLE 1.1 COMMON TECHNIQUES AND METHODS USED IN BIOCHEMISTRY

TECHNIQUE	DESCRIPTION	PURPOSE
Cell culture techniques	The growing of microorganisms, cells, or tissues in a specially prepared nutrient medium	Obtaining specific material for study
Microscopy	Magnification of structures too small to be seen by the naked eye	Visualization and identification of tissues, cells, and biomolecules
Centrifugation	Mechanical separation of mixtures placed in compartments spun about a central axis to separate components of different weights	Separation of the components of a mixture
Chromatography	Separation method that uses columns filled with gels that separate a mixture of molecules into individual components by size or charge	Purification of biomolecules
Electrophoresis	Separation of large, charged molecules in an electric field across a porous medium	Identification of the components of a mixture
Spectroscopy	Study of molecular or atomic structure by observation of its interaction with electromagnetic radiation	Identification and characterization of biomolecules
Kinetic experiments	Measurement of the rate at which a biochemical reaction yields a product	Understanding the nature and/or function of a reaction
Radioisotope labeling	Incorporation of a radioactive label into a compound	Characterization of biomolecular components; tracing reaction pathways
X-ray crystallography	Use of X-rays to record the structure of a molecule crystal	Identification of the atomic constituents of a biomolecule and of its 3D structure
Nuclear magnetic resonance (NMR)	Monitoring of the response of protons to radiation when placed in a magnetic field	Identification of the 3D structure of biomolecules in solution
Molecular modeling	Computer programs that allow the visualization of the structure of a biomolecule and the modeling of their properties	Used to investigate the properties of biomolecules when experimental techniques can not be used

study of how biomolecules pass into and out of cells, and signal transduction, the study of how cells communicate with each other and produce chemical signals inside cells. No matter what the area of specialization, biochemistry basically applies the tools of biology, chemistry, physics, and mathematics using special techniques, many of which are summarized in Table 1.1.

THE BIOCHEMISTRY-MEDICINE CONNECTION

The **genes** of living organisms are the basic units of heredity. They consist of a nucleic acid called deoxyribonucleic acid (DNA), the large biomolecule that stores the information required for the development and growth of a living organism. In humans, DNA codes for hereditary characteristics such as hair color, eye color, and height, among many other traits. Molecular genetics is the science of how DNA is copied and passed on from generation to generation and how the genetic information encoded into a DNA sequence is used in organisms to produce proteins. Anything that interferes with the copying of the DNA information or with the genes or chromosomes may cause a genetic disease. Biochemistry is routinely applied to the understanding of human genetic diseases. For example, biochemists have discovered special enzymes, called DNA polymerases, that can copy and, at times, even repair damaged DNA.

Sickle-cell anemia is a disease of the blood that affects **hemoglobin**. Hemoglobin is the iron-containing protein in red blood cells that carries oxygen throughout the body. Normal red blood cells are shaped like doughnuts with soft, hollow centers. In sickle-cell anemia, the red blood cells clump together and become sticky and stiff, adopting a curved, "banana" shape that impairs the ability of hemoglobin to efficiently carry oxygen.

The disease is caused by a **mutation** of a gene that controls hemoglobin production. A hemoglobin molecule consists of two types of amino acid chains: alpha chains and beta chains. At the molecular level, the sickle-cell anemia mutation involves the replacement of one amino acid in the beta chains by another

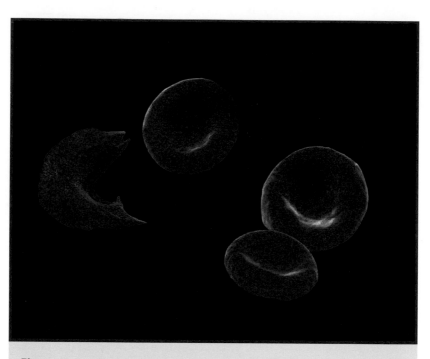

Figure 1.3   The round cells are normal red blood cells. The mis-shapen cell on the left is a sickle cell. Sickle cells clump together and impair blood circulation and the ability of blood to carry oxygen to body tissues.

incorrect amino acid. By measuring the ability of normal and sickle-cell hemoglobin to bind oxygen, biochemists were able to describe the effect of the mutation: less oxygen delivery to the tissues.

Atherosclerosis is a disease that involves the accumulation of lipid-containing molecules in large arteries, which causes inflammation and a narrowing of the arteries that may eventually lead to heart attacks. Biochemistry contributes significantly to understanding the details of the disease, for example by identifying the molecules involved in clogging blood vessels and how they travel in the body. Recent biochemical tests were also able to show that high amounts of copper and iron were present in these molecules, suggesting that these minerals, required by the body to maintain health, may not be beneficial in older people.

THE LIMEYS OF THE BRITISH NAVY

In 1747, James Lind, a Scottish naval surgeon, discovered that an unknown nutrient in citrus fruit prevented scurvy, a disease that causes weakness, spontaneous bleeding, loose teeth, pain in the joints, and finally sudden death. Before the invention of refrigeration, scurvy was a common and deadly disease typically afflicting sailors, who could only eat dry foods during their long-distance sea journeys. According to Lind, more British sailors were lost to scurvy than to war. However, very sick men would recover in a week or two after reaching land, where they could eat fresh fruit, which prompted Lind's experiments. As a result, the British Admiralty decided to distribute lemon juice to the fleet in 1795. This led to British sailors being derisively nicknamed "Limeys" because the relationship between fresh fruit and the prevention of scurvy was not common knowledge.

Understanding why fresh fruit could prevent or reverse scurvy only happened two centuries later, following the discovery of vitamin C by Albert Szent-Györgyi, a Hungarian biochemist. Szent-Györgyi was able to purify and isolate a compound that he named hexuronic acid, now known as ascorbic acid, or vitamin C. This very important substance has the chemical formula $C_6H_8O_6$. For his discovery, Szent-Györgyi was awarded the Nobel Prize for Medicine or Physiology in 1937.

Diabetes is a disease in which the body is either unable to produce enough insulin or the cells cannot use the insulin to remove **glucose** from the blood. Diabetes affects the cells of the body in many ways. Over the past several decades, biochemical techniques have been used to describe precisely how the body breaks down sugars and what can interfere with the process. The monitoring of the blood's sugar levels also involves standard biochemical tests used by physicians to get a general idea of how diabetic patients are reacting to their recommended diet, exercise, and medicinal plan, and whether or not any changes need to be made.

WHERE THERE IS LIFE, THERE IS BIOCHEMISTRY

Biochemistry is important in many fields of science in addition to medicine. For instance, biochemists investigate food by studying molecules such as vitamins, amino acids, **fatty acids**, various minerals, and water, all of which are dietary requirements for healthy nutrition. They also explain how these nutrients are absorbed by the body and what they do in the cells. For example, the question of how the body derives energy from dietary fats and oils involves a series of biochemical reactions explained by the biochemistry of the **metabolic pathways**.

One of the major scientific discoveries of the twentieth century involved working out the full chemical nature of all human genes. The Human Genome Project reached this goal in 2003. Many previously unknown genes were identified, and the identification of their protein products now involves intense biochemical research in new areas, such as comparing the proteins associated with specific genes under different conditions; using computers to explore information about genes, nucleic acids, and proteins; and using microorganisms or proteins to perform specific industrial or manufacturing processes. Biochemistry has always been an exciting area of study, but these recent advances now make it one of the most challenging sciences.

Amino Acids

Amino acids are the building blocks of proteins, the biomolecules found in all living organisms. Amino acid molecules can join together to form chains called **peptides**. Long peptides, containing more than 50 amino acids, are called **polypeptides**. *Poly* is from the Greek word that means "many," therefore, a polypeptide is made up of many amino acid chains. Amino acids all contain **carbon** (C), **oxygen** (O), **nitrogen** (N), and **hydrogen** (H).

There are 20 standard amino acids. All share a chemical core of the same **atoms**: they all have a **carboxyl group** (COOH), an **amine group** (NH_2) (also called the **amino group**), and a hydrogen atom attached to the same carbon atom. This carbon is called the alpha carbon. Amino acids can be grouped into families that have similar chemical properties. This is achieved by attaching different groups, called R groups, to the alpha carbon. The R groups of the 20 standard amino acids are

THE ELEMENTS OF LIFE

An **element** is a pure substance that cannot be broken down into simpler substances by ordinary chemical techniques. Elements combine with one another in different amounts to form everything from air, to food, to tools, to the human body.

Elements have names and chemical symbols. For example, the chemical symbol for iron is Fe, and that of oxygen is O. When we say that a substance is "pure," we mean that it contains only one kind of atom. For example, a piece of pure iron contains only atoms of the element iron, Fe. It can be heated to high temperatures and melted. Whether melted into a liquid or a solid, the Fe atoms are the same. Yet if left exposed to air, the iron will rust because it will chemically react with the oxygen in the air, forming compounds called iron oxides that contain both iron and oxygen. The chemical reaction that causes rust is called oxidation, and the iron oxide (Fe_2O_3) is the resulting reddish brown layer. The iron in the rusted layer is no longer pure because it has reacted with oxygen.

There are some 118 known elements, but only 4 elements make up 99% of living organisms. These elements are hydrogen (H), oxygen (O), nitrogen (N), and carbon (C), and they are special because they are widely available everywhere and also suitable for the chemistry of life.

Carbon (C) is sometimes called the single most important element to life because the chemical properties of the carbon atom make it ideal for building large biological molecules. Oxygen (O) is important for life, because it is required for cellular respiration, the energy-releasing reactions that sustain life. Nitrogen (N) is a major component of proteins, without which life could not exist. Almost 80% of the air is made up of nitrogen. In the plant kingdom, nitrogen is one of the three main elements that make plant life possible (the other two are potassium and phosphorus). Hydrogen (H) is the fourth most abundant element. It is almost always bound to the carbon that living systems are made of, and many chemical reactions that make life possible involve the hydrogen ion.

TABLE 2.1 STANDARD AMINO ACIDS

The table shows a list of the 20 standard amino acids and the abbreviations of their names, which can be a 3-letter code or a single letter. For example, alanine can be called "Ala" or simply "A."

AMINO ACID	3-LETTER CODE	1-LETTER CODE	R GROUP
alanine	Ala	A	$-CH_3$
arginine	Arg	R	$-(CH_2)HNBNHNH_2$
asparagine	Asn	N	$-CH_2CONH_2$
aspartic acid	Asp	D	$-CH_2COOH$
cysteine	Cys	C	$-CH_2SH$
glutamine	Gln	Q	$-CH_2CH_2CONH_2$
glutamic acid	Glu	E	$-CH_2CH_2COOH$
glycine	Gly	G	$-H$
histidine	His	H	$-CH_2C_3NHN$
isoleucine	Ile	I	$-CHCH_3CH_2CH_3$
leucine	Leu	L	$-CH_2CH(CH_3)_2$
lysine	Lys	K	$-(CH_2)_4NH_{3+}$
methionine	Met	M	$-CH_2CH_2SCH_3$
phenylalanine	Phe	F	$-C_6H_5$
proline	Pro	P	$-CH_2CH_2CH_2$
serine	Ser	S	$-CH_2OH$
threonine	Thr	T	$-COOH(CH_3)$
tryptophan	Trp	W	$-CH_2C_2NHC_6H_4$
tyrosine	Tyr	Y	$-CH_2C_6H_4OH$
valine	Val	V	$-CH(CH_3)_2$

listed in the fourth column of Table 2.1. For example, the chemical **formula** for alanine (Ala) is $C_3H_7NO_2$ and the structural formula is

$$CH_3-C\ H-COOH$$
$$|$$
$$NH_2$$

Like all other amino acids, the alpha carbon has a **bond** to a COOH group and another to a NH_2 group. But unlike the others,

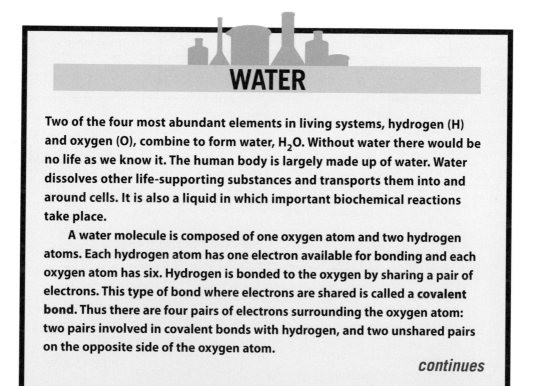

$$R - \underset{\underset{\displaystyle H}{|}}{\overset{\overset{\displaystyle NH_2}{|}}{C}} - \underset{\underset{\displaystyle OH}{|}}{C}=O$$

© Infobase Publishing

Figure 2.1   Amino acids are the building blocks of protein. All amino acids have an alpha carbon linked to an amino group, a carboxylic group, a hydrogen atom, and an R group.

its R group is **CH$_3$**. Amino acids are **acids** because they can release H$^+$ (hydrogen ions) in water at both the carboxylic and amino groups.

WATER

Two of the four most abundant elements in living systems, hydrogen (H) and oxygen (O), combine to form water, H$_2$O. Without water there would be no life as we know it. The human body is largely made up of water. Water dissolves other life-supporting substances and transports them into and around cells. It is also a liquid in which important biochemical reactions take place.

A water molecule is composed of one oxygen atom and two hydrogen atoms. Each hydrogen atom has one electron available for bonding and each oxygen atom has six. Hydrogen is bonded to the oxygen by sharing a pair of electrons. This type of bond where electrons are shared is called a **covalent bond**. Thus there are four pairs of electrons surrounding the oxygen atom: two pairs involved in covalent bonds with hydrogen, and two unshared pairs on the opposite side of the oxygen atom.

continues

continued from page 12

What makes water very special is that it is a **polar** molecule, meaning that the two sides of a water molecule have different electrical charges. There is a partial negative charge near the oxygen atom due to the unshared pairs of electrons. The hydrogen atoms have slightly positive charges because the electrons shared in the covalent bonds are pulled more toward the oxygen. Compared to hydrogen, oxygen is an **electronegative**, or electron-loving, atom. When more water molecules are in contact, the partial positive charge near the hydrogen atoms attracts the partial negative charge near the oxygen of another water molecule. This is called a **hydrogen bond** (or H bond). The ability of other charged and polar molecules to dissolve in water is due to the **polarity** of water. Because of its polarity, water is a very good solvent. Charged or polar molecules, such as salts, sugars, and amino acids, dissolve readily in water. Such compounds are said to be **hydrophilic** (water loving). Uncharged or nonpolar molecules, such as lipids, do not dissolve well in water and are said to be **hydrophobic** (water hating).

Many other important properties of water are due to its special ability to form H bonds. For example, ice floats because hydrogen bonds hold water molecules farther apart in a solid than in a liquid, where there is one less hydrogen bond per molecule. The hydrophobic effect, or the exclusion of compounds containing carbon and hydrogen (nonpolar compounds), is another special property of water caused by H bonds. The hydrophobic effect is very important in the formation of cell membranes, which are made up of long carbon-hydrogen chains. Water helps them to form by "squeezing" the nonpolar carbon chains together.

During chemical reactions, molecular parts ranging from tiny subatomic particles, such as electrons, to entire atoms, such as hydrogen, get shuffled around, transferred, shared, or exchanged. Because water is the most common chemical solvent on the Earth, such reactions mostly occur in water. However, water is not simply a passive liquid in which chemical reactions occur. In fact, it plays an active role, constantly making and breaking chemical bonds around reactive molecules in order to shuttle them from one compound to another.

continues

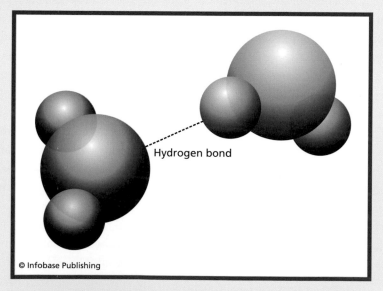

continued from page 13

Water is also important because when it dissociates, or splits, into ions, it forms:

$$H_2O \rightarrow H^+ + OH^-$$

Two water molecules ionize as follows:

$$2H_2O \rightarrow H_3O^+ + OH^-$$

The charged H_3O^+, which is called a **hydronium ion**, and OH^-, which is called a **hydroxide ion**, form stronger H bonds with surrounding water molecules. The amount of H_3O^+ will also control the **pH** of a solution. At pH 7.0, a solution is neutral—it is neither acid nor basic. At a lower pH (1–6), it has a lot of H_3O^+ and is acidic, meaning that it can release H^+ or H_3O^+. At higher pH (8–14), a solution is basic, meaning that it has little H^+ or H_3O^+ and can accept more of these ions.

Hydrogen bond

© Infobase Publishing

Figure 2.2   Above, two water molecules are linked by a hydrogen bond. This occurs due to the attraction of the slightly positive hydrogen atoms of one molecule to the slightly negative oxygen atom of another molecule.

$$^+H_3N - \overset{\overset{\textstyle H}{|}}{\underset{\underset{\textstyle R}{|}}{C_\alpha}} - \overset{\overset{\textstyle O}{\|}}{C} - \overset{\overset{\textstyle H}{|}}{N} - \overset{\overset{\textstyle H}{|}}{\underset{\underset{\textstyle R}{|}}{C_\alpha}} - \overset{\overset{\textstyle O}{\|}}{C} - \overset{\overset{\textstyle H}{|}}{N} - \overset{\overset{\textstyle H}{|}}{\underset{\underset{\textstyle R}{|}}{C_\alpha}} - \overset{\overset{\textstyle O}{\|}}{C} - \overset{\overset{\textstyle H}{|}}{N} - \overset{\overset{\textstyle H}{|}}{\underset{\underset{\textstyle R}{|}}{C_\alpha}} - \overset{\overset{\textstyle O}{\|}}{C} - \overset{\overset{\textstyle H}{|}}{N} - \overset{\overset{\textstyle H}{|}}{\underset{\underset{\textstyle R}{|}}{C_\alpha}} - \overset{\overset{\textstyle O}{\|}}{C} - O^-$$

© Infobase Publishing

Figure 2.3 In a polypeptide of five amino acids, the bold black C is the alpha carbon. The amino acids are linked together by a peptide bond (*red atoms*) linking the carboxylic group of one amino acid to the amino group of the next amino acid. The R group (*blue R*) can be any sidechain. The C_α-C-N-C_α-C-N-C_α-C-N is the "backbone."

The Peptide Bond

Amino acids are linked together by a type of bond called a **peptide bond**. A peptide bond, $-C=ONH-$, is formed between the carboxyl group of one amino acid and the amino group of another amino acid.

Small peptides consist of a few amino acids. An example is Ala-Met-Gly, a peptide consisting of alanine, methionine, and glycine. The simplest peptide is called a dipeptide, and it contains a single peptide bond formed between the C atom of the carboxyl group of one amino acid and the N atom of the amino group of the second. In a polypeptide consisting of, for instance, 58 amino acids, there are 56 peptide bonds. The C_α-CO-N-C_α-CO-N-C_α-CO-N atoms of a peptide chain, without the R groups, is called the "backbone."

The C–N peptide bond has an interesting property: It is planar and very rigid. This special geometry of the peptide bond makes it very stable and ideal to maintain the structure of proteins.

Proteins and Nucleic Acids

How do proteins function to maintain life? How do they grow? How do they recognize each other? How does the structure of DNA help explain how genetic information is encoded? Before answering such questions, it is important to understand what proteins and nucleic acids are.

PROTEIN STRUCTURE

Proteins come in many different sizes and shapes. For example, cytochrome c, a protein that transfers **electrons**, has only one polypeptide chain of 104 amino acids. Yet myosin, the protein that makes muscles contract, has two polypeptide chains with some 2,000 amino acids each, connected by four smaller chains. It is called a **multimeric** protein. No matter their size, all proteins have a **primary**, **secondary**, and **tertiary structure**. Some also have **quaternary structure**.

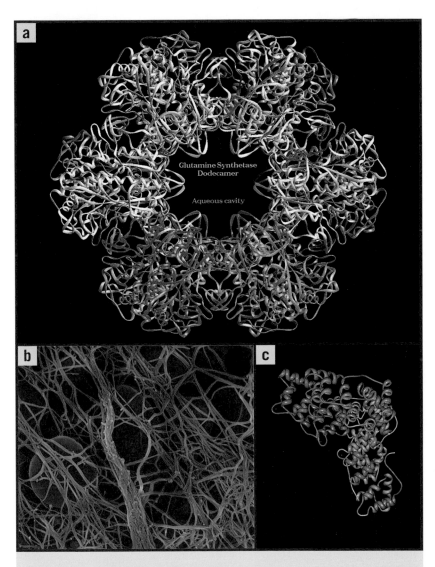

Figure 3.1   Proteins come in different shapes and sizes: (a) the enzyme glutamine synthetase, (b) the protein fibrin, and (c) the calcium pump protein.

Primary Structure

Proteins are composed of any combination of the 20 different amino acids. The amino acids are linked together by peptide bonds.

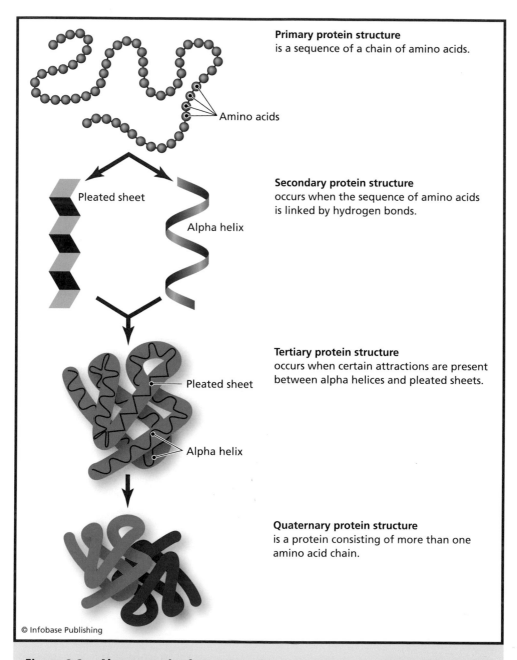

Primary protein structure
is a sequence of a chain of amino acids.

Amino acids

Secondary protein structure
occurs when the sequence of amino acids
is linked by hydrogen bonds.

Pleated sheet

Alpha helix

Tertiary protein structure
occurs when certain attractions are present
between alpha helices and pleated sheets.

Pleated sheet

Alpha helix

Quaternary protein structure
is a protein consisting of more than one
amino acid chain.

© Infobase Publishing

**Figure 3.2   Above are the four types of protein structures. All proteins have a
primary, secondary, and tertiary structure. Some have a quaternary structure as
well.**

The primary structure of a protein is the sequence of its amino acids. For example, the first 10 amino acids in the cytochrome c sequence are Ala-Ser-Phe-Ser-Glu-Ala-Pro-Gly-Asn-Pro, while the first 10 amino acids in the myosin sequence are Phe-Ser-Asp-Pro-Asp-Phe-Gln-Tyr-Leu-Ala. Therefore, the primary structure is just the full sequence of amino acids in the polypeptide chain or chains. Finding the primary structure of a protein is called **protein sequencing**. The first protein to be sequenced was the **hormone** insulin.

Secondary Structure

The polypeptide chains of proteins do not remain in a flat plane. Instead, as a protein is formed, the polypeptide chain starts to twist and curl up. It folds and coils like a rope that can be bundled in many different shapes. This coiling and folding determines the protein's secondary structure. The secondary structure is maintained by chemical bonds between the carboxyl groups and the amino groups in the polypeptide backbone. There are many secondary structure patterns, but the two most common are the α–helix, and the β–sheet.

The α-helix

The α–helix (alpha helix) has a rod shape. The peptide is coiled around an imaginary cylinder and held in shape by H-bonds formed between components of the peptide bonds.

Because there are so many H-bonds in an α–helix, this structure is very stable and strong. Helices are common structures found in most proteins.

The β-sheet

Another folding pattern is the β–sheet (beta sheet). In this arrangement, the amino acid chain zig-zags back and forth and adopts the shape of a sheet of paper. Once again it is held together by H-bonds.

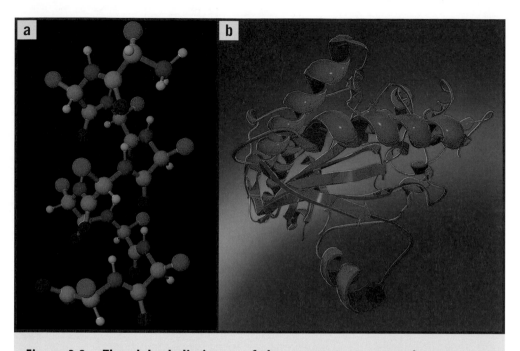

Figure 3.3 **The alpha helix is one of the most common secondary structure patterns. Pictured here are (a) the molecular structure of the alpha helix and (b) a protein consisting of several spiraling alpha helices.**

Tertiary Structure

Once it has started folding, the protein eventually tightens into a specific three-dimensional shape, called its tertiary structure. Just like humans have unique sets of fingerprints, every protein has a unique tertiary structure, which is responsible for its properties and function. The tertiary structure is held together by bonds between the R groups of the amino acids in the protein, and so depends on the amino acid sequence. There are three kinds of bonds involved in tertiary protein structure:

1. H bonds, which are weak. Since they are easy to break and reform, they make a protein flexible.
2. Ionic bonds between R groups with positive or negative charges, which are quite strong.

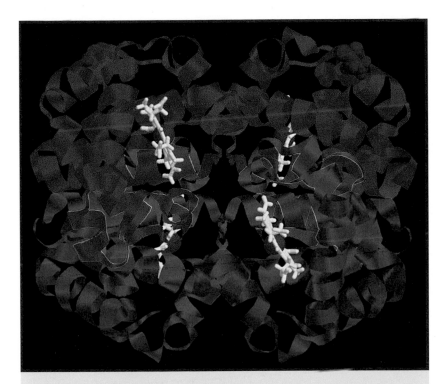

Figure 3.4 Hemoglobin transports oxygen and has a quaternary structure that shows how the chains arrange to form the molecule. As shown above, it consists of four polypeptide chains—two identical alpha globin *(blue)* and two identical beta globin *(yellow)*—each carrying a heme group *(white)* with a central iron atom, which bonds to oxygen. The green structure represents the amino acid glutamic acid at residue 6 on the beta chain.

3. **Disulfide** bridges, the S-S **bonds** between two cysteine amino acids, which are also strong.

Thus, the secondary structure is due to H bonds between backbone atoms and is independent of primary sequence; the tertiary structure is due to bonds between R-group atoms and thus depends on the amino acid sequence. For **monomeric proteins**, which have only one amino acid chain, the tertiary structure completes the three-dimensional description.

Quaternary Structure

Proteins that have more than one polypeptide chain require a higher level of organization. In the quaternary structure, the different chains are packed together to form the overall three-dimensional structure of the protein. The individual polypeptide chains can be arranged in a variety of shapes as part of the quaternary structure.

Globular or Fibrous Structures

The final three-dimensional shape of a protein can be classified as globular or fibrous. Globular means round, like a ball. Most proteins are globular, including enzymes, membrane proteins, and storage proteins. Fibrous proteins are elongated and look more like ropes. Most have structural roles, such as collagen, the main support of skin and bones. Fibrous proteins are usually composed of many polypeptide chains. Some proteins have both fibrous and globular components; for example, the muscle protein myosin has a long fibrous tail and a globular head.

PROTEINS DO EVERYTHING

Proteins are involved in all life processes in many different roles. The human body makes about 50,000 different kinds of protein, and each has a specific function.

The function of proteins depends on their structure. For example, hemoglobin, the oxygen-carrying protein in red blood cells, consists of four chains. Each chain contains one iron atom and can bind one molecule of oxygen. Since the body needs different amounts of oxygen, the structure of hemoglobin makes it easy to vary its capacity to bind oxygen and respond to what the body needs. **Immunoglobulins** are proteins that function as antibodies, which help the body fight disease and destroy foreign invaders. Antibodies have four polypeptide chains arranged in a Y-shape. This shape allows antibodies to link foreign substances together, causing them to clump and lose their ability to harm the body.

Actin is one of the proteins found in muscle. It consists of many polypeptide chains arranged in a double helix to form long filaments that are very strong. Tubulin is a protein that forms assemblies in the form of hollow tubes called microtubules. The microtubules make up cilia and flagella. Cilia are the short, hairlike structures that allow some single-cell organisms to move and help transport materials in larger organisms. In humans, cilia in the trachea, or windpipe, move mucus out of the lungs. Flagella are the whiplike "tails" that propel sperm cells, as well as some one-celled organisms.

FOOD DELIVERY

The human body contains trillions of cells that require a constant supply of nourishment, which is supplied by the food we eat. As it passes through the digestive system, food is broken down to simpler molecules usable by body cells. These final breakdown products of digestion enter the bloodstream and are carried to all the cells of the body. Water-soluble nutrients, such as sugars and salts, travel in the liquid blood and are absorbed by cells along the way. Other nutrients, however, are not very soluble in water, so special carriers are needed to deliver them to hungry cells. Serum albumin is such a carrier. It carries fatty acids, which are the building blocks of lipids, the molecules that form the membranes around and inside cells. Fatty acids are also important sources of energy, and the body maintains a storage of fatty acids in the form of fat. When the body needs energy or building materials, fat cells release fatty acids into the blood.

Serum albumin is the most plentiful protein in blood plasma. Each molecule can carry seven fatty acid molecules. They bind in deep crevices in the protein, burying their carbon-rich chains away from the surrounding water. Serum albumin also binds to many other water-insoluble molecules. In particular, serum albumin binds to many drug molecules and can strongly affect the way they are delivered through the body.

TABLE 3.1 PROTEIN FUNCTION

FUNCTION	PROTEIN	WHERE FOUND
Maintain structure	Collagen Keratin Actin	Bone, cartilage Hair, fingernails Muscle
Transport	Hemoglobin (oxygen) Transferrin (iron) Cytochromes (electrons)	Blood Liver, blood Tissues
Pumps	Sodium or potassium pumps	Cell membranes
Movement	Myosin	Muscle
Hormones	Insulin	Blood
Receptors	Rhodopsin (light)	Eye retina
Antibodies	Immunoglobulins	Blood
Storage	Myoglobin (oxygen) Albumin	Muscle Eggs, blood
Blood clotting	Thrombin Fibrinogen	Blood
Lubrication	Glycoproteins	Joints
Gateways	Porin	Cell membrane

NUCLEIC ACIDS

An enormous amount of information is required for the production of all the proteins in the body. This information is contained in very large molecules called nucleic acids. The backbone of a nucleic acid is made of alternating sugar and phosphate molecules bonded together in a long chain. Each of the sugar groups in the backbone is attached to a third type of molecule, a nitrogen **base**. Just as there are 20 amino acids that make up proteins, five different bases are found in nucleic acids: uracil (U), cytosine (C), thymine (T), adenine (A), and guanine (G).

The nitrogen base, sugar, and phosphate group collectively make up a **nucleotide**. Since there are five different kinds of bases, there are five different kinds of nucleotides. Each nucleic acid

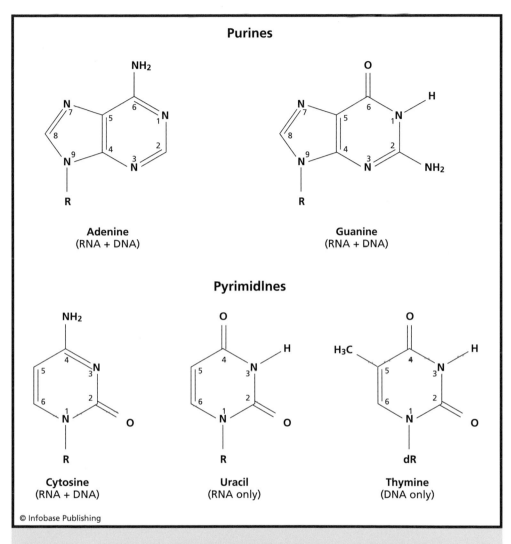

Purines

Adenine
(RNA + DNA)

Guanine
(RNA + DNA)

Pyrimidlnes

Cytosine
(RNA + DNA)

Uracil
(RNA only)

Thymine
(DNA only)

© Infobase Publishing

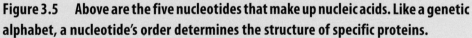

Figure 3.5   Above are the five nucleotides that make up nucleic acids. Like a genetic alphabet, a nucleotide's order determines the structure of specific proteins.

contains millions of nucleotides. The order in which they are linked is the code for the genetic information that the nucleic acid carries. In other words, the nucleotides are like a genetic alphabet, and their order determines the structure of specific proteins. Every cell in the body contains this information. There are many different types of nucleic acids that help cells replicate and build proteins. The best known are DNA and RNA.

DNA

In most living organisms, except **viruses**, genetic information is stored in a molecule called deoxyribonucleic acid, or DNA. It gets its name from the sugar group that it contains, deoxyribose. DNA is made and found in the **nucleus** of living cells. The four nucleotides found in DNA are: adenine (A), cytosine (C), guanine (G), and thymine (T). These nucleotides form two long chains that twist around each other in a spiral shape called a double helix.

The double helix has the ability to wind and unwind so that the nucleic acid chain can duplicate itself. That duplication process happens every time a cell divides.

The nucleotides in one strand of the double helix bond to nucleotides in the other strand. This is called base-pairing. This bonding is highly specific, because adenine nucleotides (A) always bond to thymine (T), and guanine (G) always bonds to cytosine (C). The double-stranded DNA molecule has a unique ability: It can make exact copies of itself, in a process called replication. When more DNA is needed, for example during reproduction or growth, the H bonds between the nucleotides break, and the two strands of the DNA molecule separate. New bases present in the cell pair up with the bases on each of the two separate strands, thus forming two new, double-stranded DNA molecules that are identical both to the original DNA molecule and to each other.

When a cell is not dividing, the DNA is not replicating and it is in the form of loose white strings in the cell nucleus. The nucleic acid strands are usually found uncoiled. To fit into the cell, the DNA is cut into shorter lengths, and each length is tightly wrapped up in a bundle called **chromatin**. During most of the life of a cell, the chromatin is dispersed throughout the nucleus and cannot be seen with a light microscope. However, when a cell starts to reproduce,

Structure of DNA

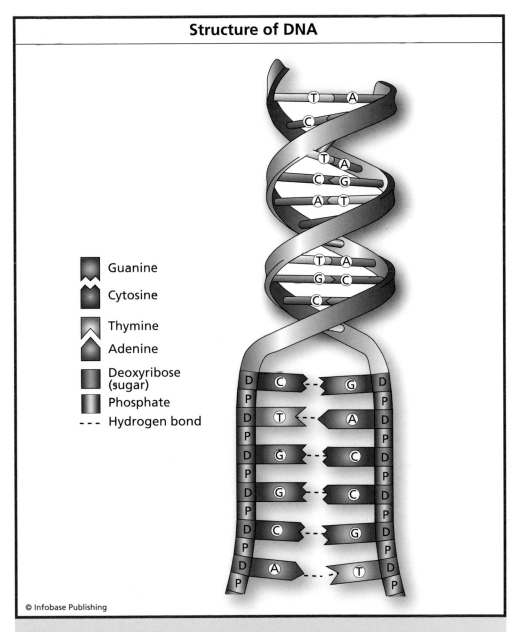

Guanine

Cytosine

Thymine

Adenine

Deoxyribose (sugar)

Phosphate

- - - Hydrogen bond

© Infobase Publishing

Figure 3.6 **A DNA molecule's structure reveals its double helix shape, made up of its four nucleotides (guanine, cytosine, thymine, and adenine) twisted together, as well as its sugar-phosphate backbone.**

DNA IS LONG

The strands of a DNA molecule are so fine that it is only possible to see them under a very powerful electron microscope. Using this instrument, a cell can be magnified 1,000 times. At this scale, the total length of the DNA in the nucleus of a cell is 3.1 kilometers (1.9 miles), about the distance between the Lincoln Memorial and the Capitol in Washington, DC.

All the genetic information of an individual is stored in the complete set of chromosomes, which is found in each cell. There are about 3 billion base pairs in the DNA in the 46 chromosomes in a human cell. The total length of DNA present in one adult human can be calculated as follows:

(Length of 1 base pair) × (Number of base pairs in a cell)
× (Number of cells in the body)
$= (0.34 \times 10^{-9} \text{ meters}) (3 \times 10^9) (10^{13})$
$= 1.0 \times 10^{13}$ m
$= 1.0 \times 10^{10}$ km

For comparison, the distance from the Earth to the Sun is 152×10^6 km. Also:

(Length of DNA in the body)/(Earth-Sun distance)
$= 2.0 \times 10^{10}$ km/152×10^6 km
$= 131$

This means that the length of the DNA in the body of an adult is as long as the distance covered by 131 trips between the Earth and the Sun.

the chromatin unwinds so that the DNA can replicate. After DNA replication, the chromatin coils up even tighter to form structures called **chromosomes**. The chromosomes are about 100,000 times shorter than fully stretched DNA, and therefore are 100,000 times thicker, so they are big enough to be seen with a light microscope.

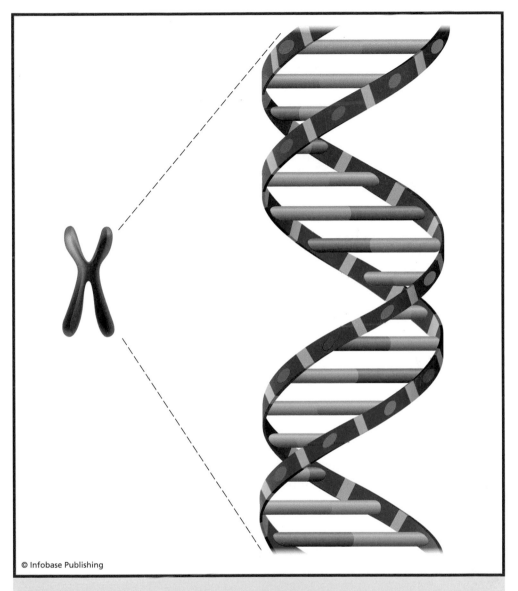

Figure 3.7 Chromosomes, which are found in the nucleus, contain DNA. When chromatin coils up tightly after DNA replication, it forms chromosomes.

In a cell that is reproducing, the chromosomes are found in pairs, with each chromosome of a pair containing one of the replicated copies of the DNA.

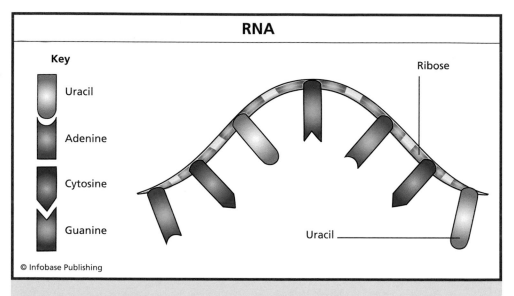

RNA

Key

Uracil

Adenine

Cytosine

Guanine

Ribose

Uracil

© Infobase Publishing

Figure 3.8 **The RNA molecule's structure is similar to the structure of DNA, except that its fourth base is uracil instead of thymine, its sugar group is ribose instead of deoxyribose, and it is composed of a single strand instead of two.**

RNA

Ribonucleic acid, or RNA, also gets its name from the sugar group it contains, in this case, ribose. In many ways, RNA is like DNA. It has a sugar-phosphate backbone with nitrogen bases attached to it, and it also contains the bases adenine (A), cytosine (C), and guanine (G). However, RNA does not contain thymine (T). Instead, the fourth base in RNA is uracil (U). Unlike DNA, RNA is a single-stranded molecule.

Various kinds of RNA function in the production of proteins in living organisms. RNA also carries the genetic information in some viruses. There are many kinds of RNA, each with its own function. For example, messenger RNA, or mRNA, carries the information stored in the cell's DNA from the nucleus to other parts of the cell where it is used to make proteins. Another kind of RNA, transfer RNA, or tRNA, binds with amino acids and transfers them to where proteins are made.

4

Enzymes

Enzymes are proteins that increase the speed of reactions by a million times or more. Without enzymes, the complex reactions in living organisms would not occur rapidly enough to support life. There are about 40,000 different enzymes in human cells, and each controls a different chemical reaction. Each kind of enzyme reacts with only one type of molecule, which is called its **substrate**. An enzyme and its substrate fit together like a lock and key. Just as a door key will open one door, enzymes make one reaction possible.

HOW ENZYMES WORK

There are four steps involved in enzyme activity:

1. An enzyme and a substrate approach each other.
2. The enzyme has a special area called the **active site**. It is an area of the enzyme that has a three-dimensional

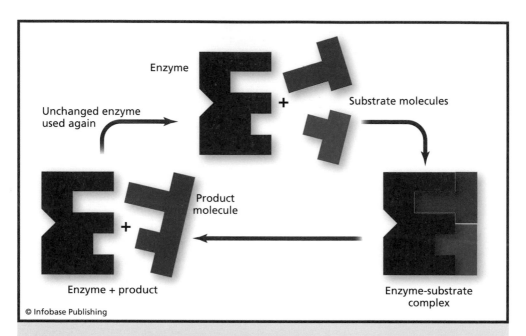

Enzyme

Unchanged enzyme used again

Substrate molecules

Product molecule

Enzyme + product

Enzyme-substrate complex

© Infobase Publishing

Figure 4.1 The above diagram illustrates the "lock and key" hypothesis of enzyme action. The approaching substrate fits perfectly into the enzyme—like a key going into a lock. The enzyme-substrate complex is then formed, and products form out of the substrate. The products no longer fit the "lock" of the active site and are released.

shape that fits the substrate precisely. The substrate bonds to the enzyme at the active site, forming an enzyme-substrate (ES) complex. Once the substrate and enzyme are bound together, the enzyme can change its shape slightly, twisting the substrate in the active site to make it more likely to change to form the product. For example, the enzyme can stretch a bond in the substrate, making it more likely to break. Enzymes can also change the conditions, such as pH, water **concentration**, and charge inside the active site and make them very different from those outside so that the reaction is more likely to happen.

3. Enzymes are **catalysts**, substances that play a role in specific chemical reactions, but which are not changed by the reaction. Thus, as a result of the enzyme-substrate reaction, the enzyme stays the same but the substrate is changed. Its shape can be different, or it can be broken down into products or combined with another molecule to make something new.

4. When the reaction is over, the enzyme and substrate separate and the enzyme, in its original condition, is ready for another reaction. But the substrate has been changed by the reaction and is now called the product.

HOW ENZYMES ARE CONTROLLED

A number of factors affect enzyme-catalyzed reactions, including temperature, pH (acidity), enzyme and substrate concentrations, and enzyme inhibitors.

Temperature   Enzymes have an optimum temperature at which they work fastest. For most enzymes, this is about 40° Celsius (104° Fahrenheit), but there are enzymes that work best at very different temperatures, such as the enzymes of the arctic snow flea that work at −10°C (14°F). If the temperature is too high, enzymes are destroyed—a process called denaturation. The heat breaks the H bonds holding the secondary and tertiary structure of the enzyme together, and therefore the enzyme and its active site lose their shape. The substrate can no longer bind, and the biochemical reaction can no longer occur.

pH levels   Just as temperature can change the shape of enzymes, the acidity of the environment does the same thing. The pH is a measure of acidity, and an increased acidity near an enzyme can cause its shape to change, again making it ineffective. All enzymes also have a pH at which they work best. For most enzymes, this is 7, the pH of most cells. A few special enzymes can work at extreme pH, such as protease enzymes in animal stomachs, which work at pH 1.

Enzyme concentration   The amount of enzyme present in a given amount of a sample is called its concentration. As the enzyme concentration increases, the rate of the reaction also increases, because there are more enzyme molecules available to drive the reaction. Yet at a certain level, the rate stops increasing, even if more enzyme is added. Normally enzymes are present in cells in rather low concentrations.

Enzyme inhibitors   **Inhibitors** are substances that lower the activity of enzymes, reducing the speed of their reactions. Some inhibitors can even completely stop enzyme-catalyzed reactions. They are found naturally, but are also produced artificially as drugs, pesticides, and other substances. The most successful inhibitors are those that have a structure very similar to that of a substrate, so that they can bind to enzyme active sites. If the active sites are occupied by an inhibitor, the enzyme is no longer available to bind its real substrate. Other inhibitors do not look like substrates. Instead, they bind on an enzyme so as to distort its shape; the geometry of the active site is changed so that the substrate no longer fits.

Effectors   A few enzymes need **effectors** to work at full capacity. Effectors are substances that increase the speed of enzyme-catalyzed reactions. They are also called "activators" because in some cases, the enzymes cannot function without them.

A FEW SPECIFIC ENZYMES

There are many different enzymes in living organisms that perform a wide variety of functions, but each will catalyze only one kind of biochemical reaction. This is called "enzyme specificity."

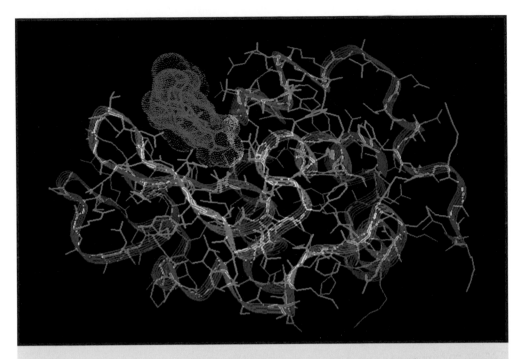

Figure 4.2   A lysozyme protects against bacterial infection by destroying the cell walls of bacteria. The above image shows the protein *(blue)* and backbone *(magenta)* of a lysozyme. It also shows the substrate *(yellow)* which is bound to the active site.

Lysozyme

A lysozyme is a small enzyme that protects living organisms from bacterial infection.

It does this by attacking the protective **cell walls** that surround each bacterial cell. **Bacteria** have a tough skin made up of long carbohydrate chains. Lysozyme breaks these chains and destroys the cell walls of bacteria. The enzyme was discovered by Alexander Fleming who was trying to make medical antibiotics, the drugs that kill bacteria. For many years, he added many different chemicals to bacterial cultures, trying to find one that would stop their growth. One day, when he had a cold, he added a drop of mucus to the culture and, to his great surprise, it killed the bacteria. Later, it was found that tears, blood, and mucus all contain lysozyme, which helps the body resist infection.

Alcohol Dehydrogenase

Alcohol dehydrogenase is much larger than lysozyme. It is an enzyme that can break down alcohol molecules. As such, it is the body's first defense line against alcohol molecules that are **toxic** for the body and can damage the nervous system. High levels of alcohol dehydrogenase are present in the body to detoxify alcohol. The enzyme does this by converting the alcohol into nontoxic molecules, such as acetate, that are easily used by cells. In this way, a dangerous molecule (alcohol) is converted by alcohol dehydrogenase into harmless foodstuff for the body. The human body has at least nine different types of alcohol dehydrogenase enzymes, each slightly different. Most of these are found in the liver and others in the lining of the stomach. Each enzyme is composed of two chains, and the different dehydrogenases can exchange their chains to create mixed enzymes that are still active. Alcohol is not the only target of these enzymes; they also make important modifications to **steroids** and fatty acids. The range of different dehydrogenases ensures that there will always be one that is perfect for the job at hand.

RNA Polymerase

Some RNAs carry genetic information from the DNA in the nucleus to the site of protein synthesis, and some RNAs transfer amino acids to the growing proteins. RNA polymerase is the enzyme that creates the different kinds of RNA molecules.

RNA polymerase is a huge enzyme with many parts, including a dozen different proteins. Together, the different parts form a factory that surrounds the DNA strands, unwinds them, and, using the information coded in the DNA chains, builds an RNA molecule. Once the enzyme gets started, it zips along the DNA, creating

RNA strands thousands of nucleotides long. RNA polymerase has to be very accurate as it copies the genetic information. To improve its accuracy, it performs a simple proofreading step as it builds an

AN ENZYME IN BUSINESS

In the United States, about 20.8 million people, or 7% of the population, have diabetes, a disease resulting from an inability of the body to regulate blood glucose levels. Fortunately, with a careful diet and medication, the many health complications of diabetes can be reduced. Part of the treatment includes the monitoring of glucose levels in the blood so that proper action may be taken when levels get too high. The enzyme glucose oxidase has now made blood glucose measurements fast, easy, and inexpensive.

Glucose oxidase is a small enzyme that converts the glucose into glucolactone, a reaction that produces hydrogen peroxide. Hydrogen peroxide is a toxic compound that can kill bacteria. This is why glucose oxidase is found on the surface of fungi, where it helps protect against bacterial infection. It is also found in honey, where it acts as a natural preservative.

This enzyme has now gone into business, becoming the center of interest of a $5 billion biotechnology industry. It is used to fabricate biosensors that measure the amount of glucose in blood. It does this by taking something that is difficult to measure—glucose—and producing something that is easy to measure—hydrogen peroxide. Glucose enters the biosensor that contains the enzyme and is converted to glucolactone. In the process, hydrogen peroxide is formed, which is then measured by a detector. The more glucose there is in the blood sample, the more peroxide is formed, and the stronger the signal at the detector.

RNA strand. It can do this because its active site can both add or remove nucleotides on the growing strand. The enzyme has the ability to remove those that are a mismatch. Overall, RNA polymerase makes an error about once in 10,000 nucleotides added, or about once per RNA strand created.

Acetylcholinesterase

Most activities of the human body involve the cells of the nervous system. The nerve cells receive signals, process them, and dispatch the information. Some nerve cells communicate directly with muscle cells, sending them the signal to contract. Other nerve cells send signals to the brain. Nerve cells communicate with each other and with muscle cells by way of substances called neurotransmitters. These are small molecules that are released from the ends of the nerve cell and that rapidly travel to neighboring cells, stimulating a response once they arrive. There are many different neurotransmitters, each with specific functions. One of the most important neurotransmitters, acetylcholine, carries signals from nerve cells to muscle cells. When certain nerve cells receive signals from the nervous system, they respond by releasing acetylcholine, which opens receptors on the muscle cells and triggers the process of contraction. Once the message is passed, the acetylcholine must be destroyed so that the contraction does not go on forever. The inactivation of the acetylcholine is the job of the enzyme acetylcholinesterase.

The enzyme reacts after a signal has passed, breaking down the acetylcholine into its two component parts, acetic acid and choline. This stops the signal, and allows the pieces to be recycled and rebuilt into new neurotransmitters for the next message.

ATP Synthase

ATP synthase is a complex enzyme, a molecular "motor," an **ion** pump, and another molecular motor all wrapped together in one amazing machine. It plays a very important role in cells, synthesizing the chemical energy-storage compound called adenosine

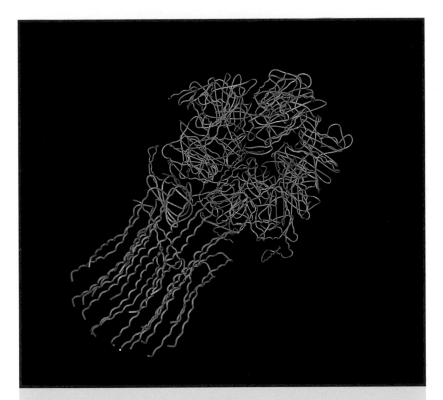

Figure 4.3   The enzyme ATP synthase synthesizes the chemical energy-storage compound known as ATP. One of this complex enzyme's two rotary motors is the F1 motor (shown in the image above), a chemical motor that creates the ATP.

triphosphate, or **ATP**. Energy released by the breakdown of ATP powers all cellular processes. ATP synthase consists of two rotary motors, each powered by a different fuel. The first motor is called F0, and it is an electric motor. It is located in the cell membrane and is powered by the flow of hydrogen ions across the membrane. As the hydrogen ions flow through the motor, they turn a circular rotor axle attached to F0. This axle is also connected to the second motor, called F1. The F1 motor is a chemical motor, and it creates the ATP. So when F0 turns, F1 turns, too, and produces ATP.

Lipids and Biological Membranes

Lipids are another type of biomolecule that are very important for life. There are many different kinds of lipids with very different chemical properties, but they all share the property of being **insoluble** in water. Examples of lipids include fats, oils, **waxes**, and steroids. Lipids make up the membranes that surround cells. Fats are one of the major food groups because of their very high energy value.

FATS

Triglycerides are the chemical form in which most fat exists in food as well as in the body. A triglyceride is made up of a three-carbon molecule called **glycerol**, which is bonded to three fatty acids. Fatty acids contain long chains of 12 to 24 carbon atoms. The carbons in fatty acids are bonded to varying numbers of hydrogen atoms.

Liquid triglycerides are called oils and are found chiefly in plants, although triglycerides from fish are also mostly oils. Triglycerides

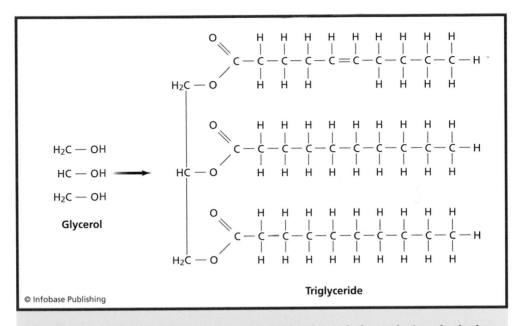

© Infobase Publishing

Figure 5.1   A triglyceride is a fat molecule that is made by replacing the hydrogens of glycerol (*left, red*) with fatty acid molecules that contain long chains of carbon atoms (*right*). When there are no carbon double bonds in the fatty acid chain, the fat is called "saturated," but when there are double bonds, as in the one shown above, it is called "unsaturated."

that are solid or semisolid at room temperature are called fats, and they are mostly found in animals. There are two kinds of fats: saturated and unsaturated. **Unsaturated fats** have at least one double bond between the carbons of the fatty acids. In a double bond, two pairs of electrons are shared by two atoms. This makes double bonds much stronger than single bonds. **Saturated fats** have no double bonds and have more hydrogens than unsaturated fats. Fats have differing properties depending on whether their fatty acids are saturated or unsaturated. For example, saturated fatty acids are typical of animal fats. This is because hibernating and migrant animals store lots of triglycerides for energy reserves. Fats have a lot of energy stored up in their molecular bonds. It is the best way to store energy for long-term use because it provides 9 **calories** per gram instead of only 4 calories per gram as sugar does. This is why the body stores fat as an energy source. When the body needs extra energy, it breaks down the stored fat. When energy from food is not needed by the body, then it is stored as fat, and when too much fat gets stored, the person becomes overweight.

Phospholipids

Phospholipids are like triglycerides, but they have two fatty acid chains called "tails" and one charged group called the "head" that contains phosphate and oxygen atoms. Because it is charged, the head is polar and therefore attracts water molecules.

The long fatty acid tail is **nonpolar** and does not attract water molecules. The polar and nonpolar parts of phospholipids allow them to form **lipid bilayers**. "Bi" is from Latin and means "two." The bilayer forms when the phospholipid molecules arrange themselves in two layers with the tails facing in (facing each other) and the heads facing out. The result is a phospholipid bilayer that has the tails buried inside and the polar atoms of the heads facing out, where they can form H bonds with water and other molecules.

The membranes of cells are composed of phospholipid bilayers through which small molecules like water and oxygen can pass. For bigger molecules, there are large proteins in the membranes that serve as channels for the transport of substances in and out of cells.

An important feature of cell membranes is that they are **semipermeable**, which means that some substances can pass through them, but others cannot. This way, a cell can control what it needs to allow in (nutrients, oxygen, water) and out (waste products from reactions).

Waxes

Waxes are also lipids with long carbon chains. In nature, they serve mostly as protective and structural coatings. Bees make wax to build the walls of honeycombs.

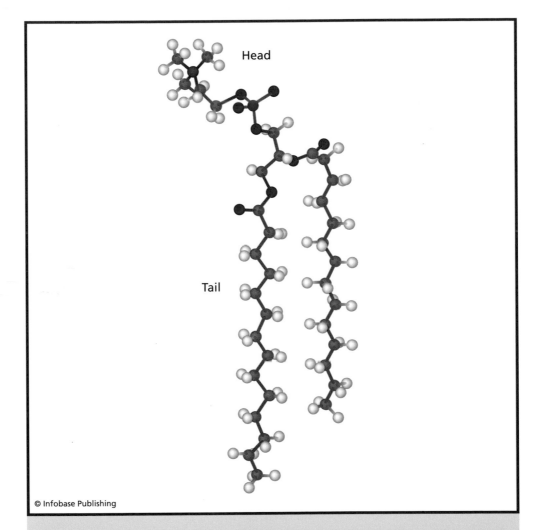

© Infobase Publishing

Figure 5.2   A phospholipid molecule is shown in the image above with a head, which has phosphate and oxygen atoms, and a tail made of two fatty acid chains. The head has atoms that are polar, or charged, and therefore they "like" water. This includes phosphate *(purple)*, oxygen *(red)*, and nitrogen *(blue)*. The tail has chains of carbon atoms *(green)* that are nonpolar, and therefore they "dislike" water.

Some plants have wax on the outside of their leaves, giving them a shiny appearance. The wax helps cut down on the evaporation of water. The feathers of birds and the fur of some animals have waxy coatings that serve as a water repellent. Humans use wax

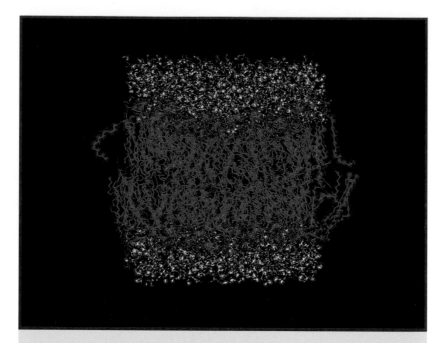

Figure 5.3 In a lipid bilayer, lipid molecules arrange themselves so that carbon tails (*green*) face each other inside the bilayer and their heads (*red and white*) face outside. The polar atoms of the lipid heads can make hydrogen bonds with water molecules.

for the same reason: They wax their skis, their cars, and the floors of their houses to protect them from water and dirt.

Steroids

Steroids are an important class of lipids. They occur in animals mostly as hormones, the chemical substances made by the body that control the activity of certain cells or organs. Steroid molecules all have a basic four-ring structure: one ring with five carbons and three rings with six carbons.

There are many kinds of steroids. **Cholesterol**, the waxy, fatty substance found in all body cells, is a sterol, meaning a combination of a lipid and a steroid. It has two main roles: First, it is a component of cell membranes, and second, it is used by the body to make hormones.

Among the many hormones in the body are the sex hormones that produce the differences between the sexes; these hormones also function in reproduction. They include testosterone, the male

WAX MATTERS

In world-class competitions such as the Olympics, the difference between winning a gold medal and watching on the sidelines often depends on a hundredth of a second. For skiers, it boils down to what type of ski wax they use to reduce the friction of skis on snow.

The type of wax used is decided by the team's wax technicians. It is their job to inspect the snow at all major competition sites. They look at the snow crystals under microscopes to determine their size and humidity. Although the snow on downhill and cross-country courses can look smooth on television, under a microscope, snow is seen to consist of crystals that have rough edges with varying water contents. The technicians create mixtures of different waxes and add other closely guarded secret ingredients that they test under different racing weather and snow conditions.

The night before the big ski event, they carefully apply the appropriate wax for the weather predicted for the next day. Since the weather can often change, they also prepare other skis with another kind of wax more suitable, say, for snow conditions that could become wetter. All these adjustments are made to reduce the friction between the skis and the snow and give the skier an edge in gaining a few milliseconds. Generally, when the temperature is very cold and the snow is hard, skiers use a hard wax to make the ski base more resistant to the sharp ice crystals. In wet snow, they use a softer wax to repel the melt water generated from the skis. Otherwise, the melt water would stick to the skis, like a glass of water sticks to a glass table, and force the skier to waste energy by working harder, with the result being the loss of an Olympic medal.

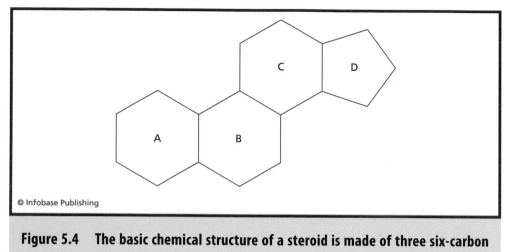

Figure 5.4   The basic chemical structure of a steroid is made of three six-carbon rings and one five-carbon ring.

hormone; estradiol, a female hormone; and progesterone, involved in pregnancy. Another class of steroids are the anabolic steroids, the muscle-growth hormones derived from testosterone. They are often abused by bodybuilders and in competitive sports. It has been shown that anabolic steroid abuse can result in a wide range of harmful side effects including some that are physically unattractive, such as acne and breast development in men. The side effects can also be life threatening, such as liver cancer and heart attacks.

Vitamins

Vitamins are nutrients that are present in small quantities in food and are essential for growth and to maintain health. There are many vitamins, and they are divided into two groups: the water-soluble vitamins that include the B vitamins and vitamin C, and the **fat-soluble** vitamins that include vitamins A, D, E, and K. The far-soluble vitamins are also lipids.

The two groups of vitamins are both needed by the body but are dissimilar in many ways. For example, cooking destroys the water-soluble vitamins much more than the fat-soluble vitamins.

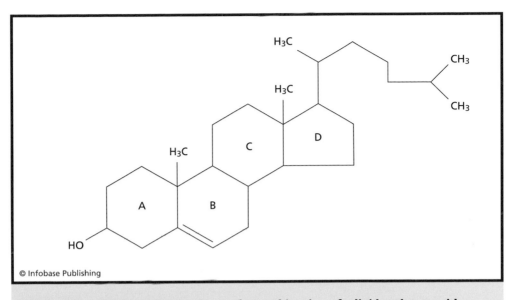

© Infobase Publishing

Figure 5.5   Cholesterol is made up of a combination of a lipid and a steroid.

Another difference is that the fat-soluble vitamins are stored by the body, just like fats, while water-soluble vitamins are easily passed in the urine. The fat-soluble vitamins can therefore accumulate to high levels that can possibly become toxic.

Vitamin A was the first vitamin discovered by biochemists almost 100 years ago. This is why it is called "A." It is essential for the normal growth and development of the body, especially the bones and teeth. It also protects mucous membranes from infection and is needed for normal vision and healthy skin and hair. Foods rich in vitamin A include milk, carrots, egg yolks, and spinach. Vitamin D, found in milk, beef, and sardines, helps the body absorb calcium to strengthen bones and teeth. Vitamin E, found in nuts, oils, and green leafy vegetables, protects cells from damage and also helps wound healing. Vitamin K, also found in some oils and green leafy vegetables, is needed for proper bone growth and is essential for the normal clotting of blood.

Carbohydrates: Energy for Living Organisms

Carbohydrates are so-called because these molecules are made up of carbon atoms ("carbo") bonded to groups of oxygen and hydrogen atoms, called hydroxide groups ("hydrate"). Carbohydrates are a major energy source for living organisms. They also have a structural role. For example, the cell walls in plants and wood are both made of a carbohydrate called **cellulose**. In fact, most of the weight of plants comes from a carbohydrate of one kind or another. Depending on their structure, they are grouped in families. The simplest sugars, such as glucose, are called **monosaccharides**. Molecules made up of two monosaccharides bonded together are called **disaccharides**. The word **saccharide** comes from the Latin *saccharum*, meaning "sugar." Molecules made up of more than two monosaccarides are called **polysaccharides**. Sugars are very soluble in water, as seen when adding a spoonful to a cup of tea.

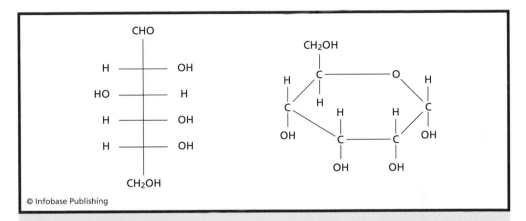

© Infobase Publishing

Figure 6.1   Glucose is a monosaccharide. It has two forms: the straight form (*left*) and the ring form (*right*).

MONOSACCHARIDES

Glucose, the most important monosaccharide, has the molecular formula $C_6H_{12}O_6$. Most carbohydrates in food are broken down to glucose in the course of digestion. Glucose is used by the body to make all the other carbohydrates it needs, such as **glycogen**, an energy-storage compound found in the liver and in muscle. Glucose can also be used in the synthesis of amino acids and other needed compounds in the body.

Other common monosaccharides are fructose, the sugar found in fruits and honey that is also used as a **preservative** in foodstuffs, and galactose, found in milk sugar. Sucrose, or table sugar, is a disaccharide made up of glucose and fructose molecules bonded together. The chemical names of sugars always end in "-ose."

POLYSACCHARIDES

Polysaccharides are large molecules that are made up of hundreds of simple sugar molecules (monosaccharides) bonded together. The most important polysaccharides are **starch**, cellulose, and glycogen.

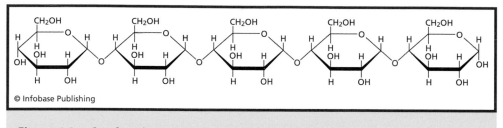

© Infobase Publishing

Figure 6.2   Amylose is a type of starch found in long grain rice.

Starch

Starch is made up of long chains of glucose molecules, and it is not soluble in water.

Plants and some algae store food in the form of starch. In plants, starch is mainly found in seeds, roots, and tubers as well as in stems, leaves, fruits, and even pollen. Grain seeds, such as corn kernels, contain up to 75% starch. Therefore, it is an important component of the carbohydrates in the diet and a very good source of energy for the body. Starch is found in foods such as cereal, pasta, and potatoes, and cornstarch is used to thicken sauces. Laundry starch is a liquid form of starch used to stiffen the collars and sleeves of shirts. An advantage of using it is that dirt and sweat will stick to the starch instead of the shirt textile fibers, with the result that "collar rings" are easily washed away with the starch.

Cellulose

Cellulose is a carbohydrate that supports or protects plants. Like starch, it is made of repeating units of glucose. The bonds between the glucose molecules in cellulose are different from the bonds in starch. This matters a great deal, because enzymes in the human body can break the bonds in starch to produce glucose, but they cannot break the cellulose bonds and make glucose from it. This is why cereal or corn (starch) can be eaten, but not wood (cellulose).

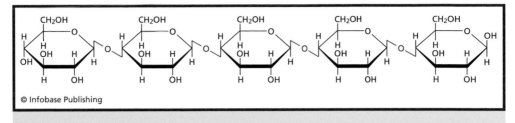

© Infobase Publishing

Figure 6.3   Cellulose is a polysaccharide used to make the cell walls in plants.

Termites can "eat wood" because they contain specific micro-organisms that, in turn, contain bacteria that actually digest the wood. These bacteria have enzymes that can break the bonds of cellulose.

Cellulose is the main structural element of the cell walls of most plants and is also a major component of wood, as well as cotton and other textile fibers, such as linen and hemp. The history of cellulose is as old as that of humankind. For instance, fine clothes and cottons have been recovered from the tombs of the ancient kings of Egypt, the pharaohs. Today, cellulose and its derivatives are used in the industrial preparation of paper and also in the chemical industry as a stabilizer, dispersing agent, thickener, and gelling agent. Cellulose is also a component of dietary fiber.

Glycogen

Just as plants store glucose as starch, animals, including humans, store glucose as glycogen. Glycogen is made and stored mainly in the liver and the muscles. Like starch and cellulose, glycogen consists of long chains of glucose molecules.

Plants make starch, and animals, in turn, eat plant materials and products. When the food is digested, the starch it contains is broken into monosaccharides. The major product is glucose, which can be broken down immediately by the body for energy or

FROM CARBOHYDRATES TO BREAD, BEER, AND WINE

Fermentation is a process that chemically converts sugar to alcohol or acids. Alcohol fermentation is done by a fungus called yeast and some kinds of bacteria. The yeast converts the glucose ($C_6H_{12}O_6$) to ethanol (C_2H_5OH) and the gas carbon dioxide (CO_2):

$$C_6H_{12}O_6 \rightarrow 2C_2H_5OH + 2CO_2$$

Humans have long taken advantage of fermentation to make bread, beer, and wine. In bread-making, the CO_2 is trapped between long protein molecules called gluten, which are present in wheat. Since CO_2 is a gas, this causes the bread to rise, just like blowing air into a balloon. The ethanol evaporates from the mixture as the bread is baked, giving it its wonderful smell. In beer and wine-making, the ethanol is collected as the desired alcohol, and the CO_2 makes these beverages effervescent (carbonated).

The carbohydrate source determines whether beer or wine is produced by fermentation. Beer is made from grains, such as barley, wheat, or rye that are allowed to germinate, producing malt. Enzymes convert the malt into sugar, which can then ferment. The flowers of a plant called hops are added to give beer its typical bitter taste. Wine is made from the sugar of grapes. After the harvest, the grapes are crushed in big vats and allowed to ferment. The resulting alcohol is wine. If red grapes are used, the wine is red, and if the grapes are white, the wine is white.

converted in the liver and muscles into glycogen for storage. When the body needs more energy, the glycogen is broken down to glucose by special enzymes.

Chitin

A polysaccharide called **chitin** is the major component in the hard outer shells of crustaceans, such as shrimps, crabs, and lobsters. A young crustacean has to shed its shell when it grows, because the chitin is hard and cannot stretch. On the other hand, chitin is very tough and provides an excellent outer protective covering.

Pectin

Pectin is a polysaccharide found in the nonwoody cell walls of plants where it binds cells together and helps the plant take in water. In fruits, it is broken down during the ripening process, and this is why ripe fruits are soft. The fruits that contain the most pectin are apples, plums, grapefruits, and oranges. Pectin is commonly used as a food additive, especially as a thickener for jams and marmalades, where it provides the jellylike consistency.

Heparin

Heparin is a complex polysaccharide consisting of repeating disaccharide subunits. It is found in the liver and the lungs. As a commercial drug, it is used to thin the blood and prevent it from clotting, for example, during surgery.

Metabolic Pathways: The Roads to Energy

Metabolism includes all the chemical reactions in a living organism. It comes from the Greek *metabolē*, meaning "change." All living things need energy for their life processes. In plants, the energy comes from sunlight. Plants also absorb mineral nutrients from the soil in which they grow. Animals derive needed energy from the breakdown of nutrients in food obtained from the environment. Enzymes can break down large carbohydrate molecules into smaller glucose molecules, which are, in turn, broken down for energy. The breakdown of food for energy is a part of metabolism.

Metabolic reactions are of two general kinds. **Catabolism** includes all reactions that break down large molecules into smaller ones with a release of energy, as in the breakdown of carbohydrates. Catabolic reactions are also called destructive metabolism.

Anabolism includes all reactions that use energy in the synthesis of larger molecules from smaller molecules, as in the production of proteins from amino acids. Anabolic reactions are also called constructive metabolism.

METABOLIC PATHWAYS

The different metabolic reactions all have one feature in common: They are very complex and occur in several steps, each step producing specific substances and each controlled by specific enzymes. All the steps from the starting compound to the final product(s) are called a metabolic pathway, because the reactions occur in a specific order and produce certain molecules. We can think of a metabolic pathway as a map that is followed to get from one point to another. This is a big advantage, because at each step, the product can take another pathway, depending on what the cell needs. Another advantage is that some of the steps are reversible, so the cell again gains flexibility in managing all of its chemicals. This is like having a choice of using different routes or streets to get to a destination, with the freedom of returning home if something was forgotten.

Digestion

Digestion is a metabolic process that features catabolic (destructive) reactions. It breaks down all food into smaller molecules that can be absorbed by the cells of the body. This is required because the molecules of which foods are made are much too large to pass into the bloodstream. After digestion, the resulting smaller molecules can enter the bloodstream and be carried to individual cells throughout the body.

The smaller end products of digestion also make up the metabolic stores, which include a pool of simple sugars, like glucose; fatty acids, which come from the breakdown of lipids or fats; and amino acids, produced by the breakdown of proteins. All the simpler molecules of the metabolic stores are readily available for anabolic (constructive) and catabolic (destructive) metabolism.

The carbohydrates, proteins, and lipids in foods are mostly in complex forms. For example, the carbohydrates are present as disaccharides, such as sucrose, or polysaccharides, such as starch. The first step in digestion is the breakdown of the larger, insoluble molecules into smaller, soluble forms that can be transported across the intestinal wall into the blood for delivery to the tissues.

The breakdown of food begins in the mouth as it is chewed. Chewing mixes saliva in the food. Saliva contains the enzyme amylase that begins the digestion of starch. Once chewed and swallowed, the food reaches the stomach, where the acid present

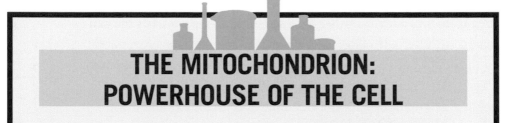

THE MITOCHONDRION: POWERHOUSE OF THE CELL

Mitochondria are found in all cells. Found in the cell **cytoplasm**, these structures are surrounded by both an inner and outer membrane. The outer membrane is fairly smooth. The inner membrane has deep folds called **cristae**, which contain electron-transport compounds. It is on the cristae that most ATP is produced in the final stage of cellular respiration. Mitochondria are called the powerhouses of the cell because they are the site of ATP production, and ATP provides the energy for most cell activities.

Mitochondria can have different shapes, depending on the kind of cell they are in. The number of mitochondria present in a cell also varies with cell type and may range from a single large mitochondrion to thousands. The region inside the inner membrane is called the matrix. This is where the **Krebs cycle** that converts pyruvate into CO_2 and energy takes place, so it contains a lot of enzymes. Mitochondria contain ribosomes, small particles composed of RNA and protein that are the sites of protein synthesis. Mitochondria also contain their own special DNA.

helps to further degrade the food. Various enzymes also become involved in the breakdown process. The proteases begin the breakdown of proteins and the lipases begin the breakdown of fats. The

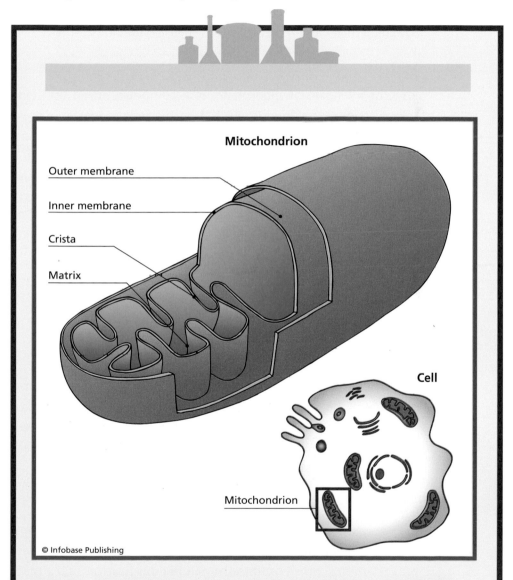

Figure 7.1   The mitochondrion is found in all cells and contains many structures. This includes the cristae, where most ATP is produced in the final stage of cellular respiration. Being the site of ATP production, the mitochondrion is called the powerhouse of the cell.

whole mixture, now called chyme, moves to the small intestine. In the small intestine, other enzymes complete the breakdown of the nutrients in food into glucose, amino acids, and fatty acids, which can be transported across the intestinal wall and into the bloodstream, which carries them to all the cells of the body.

ATP

ATP, or adenosine triphosphate, is a compound used by living things to store the energy released by the breakdown of glucose and other compounds. ATP is formed when a smaller compound called ADP, or adenosine diphosphate, combines with a **phosphate group**. A phosphate group (Pi) contains four oxygens bonded to phosphorus. To combine with a phosphate group, ADP needs energy:

$$ADP + Pi + energy \rightarrow ATP$$

The reverse reaction produces ADP and releases energy:

$$ATP \rightarrow ADP + energy + Pi$$

In cells, the energy needed to make ATP comes from glucose, glycogen, fatty acids, etc. When an ATP molecule is produced, it contains chemical energy in a form and quantity that can be used by the cell. So, when a cell needs energy, it can get it from the breakdown of stored ATP.

THE ENERGY PATHWAY: CELLULAR RESPIRATION

All living cells produce energy by a process called **cellular respiration**. It involves a series of metabolic pathways, each with several reactions. Most commonly, cellular respiration takes place in the presence of oxygen and involves the breakdown of glucose to carbon dioxide and water, coupled with the production of ATP.

Aerobic respiration occurs when oxygen is available, and anaerobic respiration occurs when there is no oxygen. The two paths of cellular respiration begin with same reactions.

Respiration With Oxygen

The aerobic pathway involves three series of reactions: **glycolysis**, the Krebs cycle, and the **electron transport chain**.

WHAT IS LACTIC ACID?

To function, the muscles of the body engage in cellular respiration using oxygen supplied by the lungs and blood. However, when muscles are working hard, as when a person is running or lifting heavy weights, the oxygen supplied by the lungs and the blood system can't get there fast enough to keep up with muscle activity. When this happens, muscles switch to lactic acid fermentation. Special enzymes become involved and convert the 3-carbon molecules of pyruvic acid into lactic acid.

When muscles work too hard, lactic acid builds up in the muscles and this is the process that makes them sore (muscle fatigue). Once muscles form lactic acid, they can't do anything else with it. Once the oxygen supply becomes adequate again, some of the lactic acid is converted back to pyruvate and broken down to carbon dioxide and water. The rest is carried away from the muscles by the blood and eventually converted by the liver back to glucose. Once the lactic acid is removed, the muscles no longer hurt. This is why rest is the best way to recover from hard work or exercise.

Some bacteria, such as the lactobacillus acidophilus found in yogurt, also carry out lactic acid fermentation. It is the presence of lactic acid in yogurt that gives it its sour taste.

During glycolysis, the 6-carbon glucose molecule is broken down in a series of steps into two molecules of a 3-carbon compound called pyruvate. There is also a net gain of two molecules of ATP from the reactions of glycolysis.

During the reactions of the Krebs cycle, pyruvate is broken down into CO_2 and water, producing another two molecules of ATP. It also produces energy molecules called **NADH** and $FADH_2$. During the final reactions of cellular respiration, NADH and $FADH_2$ are used to make more ATP.

The reactions of the electron transport chain yield most of the ATP produced by cellular respiration. These reactions take place in tiny structures within the cell called mitochondria and involve the transport of electrons. The end result of the electron transport chain is the production of 32 molecules of ATP. Thus, the total breakdown of one glucose molecule to carbon dioxide and water yields 36 molecules of ATP.

Respiration Without Oxygen

Anaerobic respiration only has two steps: glycolysis and **fermentation**. Glycolysis again converts glucose into pyruvate. But in the absence of oxygen, fermentation converts pyruvate into **ethanol**, lactic acid, or a variety of other products, depending on the organism involved.

The ability of cells to produce energy without oxygen is very important. For example, when high levels of oxygen are used, such as during prolonged vigorous exercise, some ATP can still be made. In anaerobic respiration, much of the energy of the original glucose is still present in the ethanol or lactic acid, the end products of fermentation.

OTHER METABOLIC PATHWAYS

All the chemical reactions that happen in a cell occur in the form of a stepwise metabolic pathway. They are all controlled by enzymes, and each product created at each step of a pathway can either be further processed down the line of that pathway or shifted to another pathway, depending on what the cell needs. Some other pathways are as follows:

Fatty acid oxidation   This pathway produces fatty acids from **oxidation** reactions.

Gluconeogenesis   This pathway produces glucose from carbon-containing molecules that are not carbohydrates. For example, it can convert pyruvate into glucose, the reverse of glycolysis.

Porphyrin pathway   This pathway creates very important molecules called **porphyrins** that are in turn used to make another molecule, called a heme, which can bind oxygen. Hemes are needed by oxygen-binding proteins like hemoglobin and **myoglobin** that transport or store oxygen.

Urea cycle   This pathway converts ammonia, a toxic nitrogen-containing waste product of protein metabolism, into another, less toxic molecule called **urea**, which can be eliminated from the body as urine.

Metabolic Disorders

Because enzymes are required in all metabolic pathway reactions, a missing or damaged enzyme may result in a metabolic disorder, meaning that the pathway can no longer produce what it should because there is an interruption in the series of required reactions. When this happens, cells may have too much of some substances or too little of others. For example, a disorder called phenylketonuria is caused by the lack of an enzyme called phenylalanine hydroxylase. The enzyme converts the amino acid phenylalanine to another amino acid, tyrosine. When the enzyme is missing, phenylalanine

BIOCHEMISTRY MILESTONES: PART I

The study of biochemistry began about 400 years ago. It was not named as such, however, until 1903 when Carl Neuber, a German chemist, realized that the chemistry of life was such an extensive field of study that it could no longer be considered a mere chemistry subsection.

As early as the late 1700s, it was known that stomach secretions were needed for the breakdown of food. It was also known that plant extracts could convert starch to sugars. However, the precise nature of these processes was not understood. It was also believed that living organisms did not obey the same laws of science as nonliving materials. For instance, it was thought that only living beings could produce the molecules of life.

In 1828, Friedrich Wöhler, a German chemist, was able to produce in the laboratory a molecule called urea, the waste product of protein breakdown in the body. This proved that compounds made by the body could also be created artificially.

Meanwhile, a French chemist, Louis Pasteur, was studying the fermentation of sugar to alcohol by yeast. Specifically, he wanted to know why some wines turn sour during fermentation. In those days, the accepted idea was that fermentation was just the breakdown of sugar into its components, which included alcohol. Pasteur first showed that fermentation needed a vital force, which he called "fragments," in the yeast. Examining the sour wine under a microscope, he saw that, unlike the good wine, it also contained rod-shaped microorganisms. To prevent souring of the wine, Pasteur heated the wine after fermentation to 50°C (122°F). Today, this heating process is called pasteurization, and it is known that the little rod-shaped organisms that heat destroys are bacteria.

In 1878, the "fragments" identified by Pasteur were named enzymes by the German physiologist Wilhelm Kühne. In 1897, Eduard Büchner, a German chemist, accidentally discovered that a yeast juice could convert sucrose to ethanol. He was able to show that the sugar was fermented even in the absence of living yeast cells in the mixture, and named the factor responsible for the fermentation of sucrose zymase. In 1907, he received the Nobel Prize in Chemistry. The 40 years of biochemical research that followed yielded the details of the chemical reactions of fermentation.

cannot produce tyrosine. Instead, phenylalanine builds up in the body and seriously affects normal brain development. The result is mental retardation.

Another example is acid lipase disease, which occurs when the enzyme acid lipase, needed to break down fats, is lacking or missing. The result is a toxic buildup of these fats in cells and tissues. These fatty substances are lipids and include waxes, oils, and cholesterol.

Porphyria is a disease that results from an inability of the body to make porphyrin rings. There are eight steps involved in their production, each requiring a specific enzyme. There are different kinds of porphyria, depending on which enzyme is missing. People affected by porphyria cannot make normal hemoglobin to carry oxygen in the blood.

Most metabolic disorders are inherited, meaning that they are passed by parents to their offspring in defective genes. Also, they have no cure. They are usually treated with medications and a special diet to provide the missing substances or remove the toxic ones that build up.

Photosynthesis: The Basis of Life on Earth

Some 3 billion years ago the Earth underwent a dramatic change. Until that time, life forms were dependent on the limited resources in the local environment, like the organic molecules made by lightning or those coming out of hot springs. However, these resources were rapidly being used up. Everything changed with the evolution of cells that could use energy from sunlight to synthesize nutrients. This new process, **photosynthesis**, eventually changed the atmosphere and made possible the enormous diversity of life forms on the Earth today. Today, photosynthesis is the foundation of life on the Earth, providing food and oxygen. In photosynthesis, plants take one form of energy (light) and transform it into a form of chemical energy that they can use: sugars. Photosynthesis means "making with light." Only plants, algae, and a few kinds of bacteria can carry out this reaction. Photosynthetic organisms use energy from sunlight to combine carbon dioxide

(CO_2) and water (H_2O) to create glucose ($C_6H_{12}O_6$). Oxygen gas (O_2) is given off as a waste product of the reaction. All the oxygen in the atmosphere has been produced by photosynthesis. The reaction is written as follows:

$$6CO_2 + 6H_2O + light \rightarrow C_6H_{12}O_6 + 6O_2$$

The carbon dioxide comes from the air, and the water comes from the soil in which the plant grows. When a plant is watered or when it rains, water enters the root and is transported to the leaves by plant cells called xylem. To protect themselves against drying out, leaves have structures called **stomata** that allow gas to enter and leave. "Stoma" is from the Greek and means "hole." Both carbon dioxide and the oxygen produced during photosynthesis pass in and out of the leaf through the opened stomata.

CHLOROPLASTS

Photosynthesis occurs inside plant cells in special structures called **chloroplasts**. Animal cells do not have chloroplasts. A typical plant cell might contain as many as 50 chloroplasts. They have a double outer membrane to protect their contents. The outer membrane is permeable, meaning that it lets molecules through. But the inner membrane is semipermeable—it contains proteins able to control which substances pass in and out. For example, the molecules needed by the chloroplast to make sugar are allowed in, and the glucose produced is allowed to leave the cell. Inside the chloroplast are other structures, the thylakoids and the grana (singular = **granum**), where photosynthesis takes place.

Chlorophyll is the green pigment that captures the light energy used for photosynthesis.

Chlorophyll is also found in green algae. Photosynthetic bacteria have a modified kind of chlorophyll called bateriochlorophyll.

All chlorophylls are composed of a flat ring of carbon atoms, called a porphyrin, that surrounds a central magnesium ion. There are two main kinds of chlorophylls, *a* and *b*. They differ in having different chemical groups attached to their porphyrin rings. The groups allow the chlorophylls to absorb different wavelengths of visible light, so that light energy that is not well absorbed by chlorophyll *a* is instead captured by chlorophyll *b*. Thus these two kinds of chlorophyll work together in absorbing energy from sunlight.

LIGHT

Light is a part of the electromagnetic spectrum, which is more familiar than one might think. In addition to visible light, the electromagnetic spectrum includes radio waves, microwaves, infrared, ultraviolet, and X-rays. The only part of the electromagnetic spectrum detectable to humans is visible light.

Sunlight, which appears colorless, is a mixture of all the colors in the visible range of the electromagnetic spectrum, from red and orange at one end, to blue and purple at the other. The colors can also be seen by shining white light through a prism that can separate it into colors. Light has wave properties, and each of these colors actually corresponds to a different wavelength of light, some longer and others shorter. Wavelength is measured as the distance between two crests of the wave; red wavelengths are longer than blue wavelengths. The longer the wavelength, the less energy the light has. Thus, there is less energy in red light and more in blue light. Wavelengths longer than the visible red light are referred to as infrared, while those shorter than violet are ultraviolet. Sunscreens protect the skin from damaging effects of ultraviolet (UV) radiation from the Sun.

Special molecules can absorb light energy from wavelengths of the visible spectrum and also release it. These molecules are called pigments, or chromophores, from the Greek *chromo* meaning "color." The main pigments in photosynthesis are the chlorophylls; they appear green because they absorb all colors (wavelengths) strongly except green, which is reflected outward. Since it is reflected, the human eye can see it. There are also other plant pigments,

The photosynthesis machinery in the chloroplasts is in a system of **thylakoid** membranes, which are stacked in arrays called grana. The grana look like a stack of coins. The thylakoid membranes contain enzymes and protein assemblies that contain the chlorophyll. The two kinds of protein assemblies are called **photosystem I** and photosystem II. These assemblies absorb energy from light.

such as carotenoids. Unlike chlorophylls, they do not absorb light from the red-orange region of the electromagnetic spectrum, so they appear red-orange. However, chlorophyll absorbs so strongly that it masks the carotenoid colors, which are much less intense than the chlorophyll green. Carotenoid colors are only revealed when the chlorophyll molecules decay in the fall. Thus, the trees turn red, orange, and golden brown.

Light

Chlorophyll

© Infobase Publishing

Figure 8.1 Chlorophyll is the green pigment that captures light energy used in photosynthesis. Chlorophyll reflects green light instead of absorbing it, which is why plants that contain chlorophyll appear green.

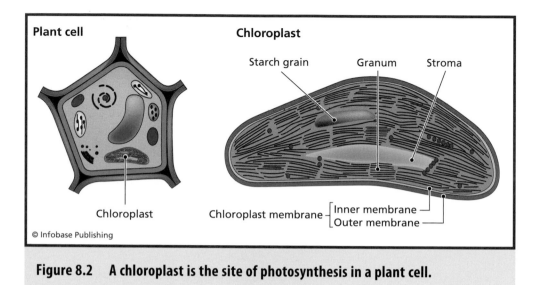

Figure 8.2   A chloroplast is the site of photosynthesis in a plant cell.

REACTIONS OF PHOTOSYNTHESIS

In the first set of reactions of photosynthesis, chlorophyll traps light energy. This energy produces some high-energy electrons in the chlorophyll. Energy from these electrons is used to produce ATP and another high-energy carrier, NADPH. In another reaction in this first stage, water is split into hydrogen and oxygen. Low-energy electrons from water replace the low-energy electrons in the chlorophyll, and the oxygen gas bubbles away. The oxygen produced by this reaction is the source of all of the oxygen in the air that we breathe.

In the second set of reactions of photosynthesis, carbohydrates are synthesized from carbon dioxide and hydrogen (from NADPH). The ATP and NADPH produced by the first set of photosynthesis reactions provide the energy for these reactions.

PHOTOSYNTHESIS AND BIOTECHNOLOGY

Biotechnology includes all technologies that use biological techniques or organisms to develop new products. Light has a big

THE DUAL NATURE OF LIGHT

Light is at the same time both a wave and a particle, and so has a dual nature. Light behaves like a wave in that it has a wavelength and a frequency. It behaves like a particle in that it can be described as traveling as small packets containing discrete amounts of energy. Particles of light are called photons. The energy in photons of sunlight absorbed by certain electrons in chlorophyll is what initiates the first stage of photosynthesis.

In a **vacuum**, light travels at a constant speed, $c = 2.998 \times 10^8$ m/s (6.7 x 10^8 mph), but it is slowed down by friction if it travels in air or water. Some important properties of light include:

Absorption: Light can be absorbed by different materials. How does this happen ? Matter Is made of atoms and all atoms vibrate along with their electrons, to an extent that depends on what kind of atoms they are. Some vibrate more than others and thus have higher energy levels. For light to be absorbed by matter, there is one condition that must be met: The frequency of the incoming light wave must be at or near the vibration energy levels of the electrons in the material. The electrons can then absorb the energy of the light wave and change their energy state.

Reflection: When the incoming light frequency does not match the vibration frequency of a material, the material will not be able to absorb the light. The electrons will just vibrate a little and send the energy back out with the same frequency as the incoming wave, just like a ball bouncing off a wall.

Refraction: Refraction occurs when light waves penetrate into a material that cannot absorb them. So they simply travel through the material and come out on the other side. But inside the material, they are slowed down, and this has the effect of bending the waves inside the material so that they pass out of the material at a different angle from the angle of entry. Light of different energies bends at slightly different angles. For instance, violet light has more energy, so it is slowed down to a greater extent than a wave of red light, and comes out more bent. This is why the order of the colors that we see in a rainbow goes from red (less energy) to violet (more energy).

advantage as an energy source: It is clean and available wherever and whenever the sun shines. Due to limited supplies of fossil fuels, such as oil and petroleum, and because of the increasing concern about harmful CO_2 emissions, the development of technologies capable of using solar energy has nowadays become a priority.

Most current solar-energy technologies use silicon materials to capture solar energy. The result is an efficient solar cell, but the

BIOCHEMISTRY MILESTONES: PART II

In 1926, James B. Sumner, an American chemist, showed that enzymes were pure proteins and that enzymes could be crystallized. The fact that pure proteins could be enzymes was definitively proven by John H. Northrop and Wendell M. Stanley, who worked on digestive enzymes. Summer, Northrop, and Stanley were awarded the 1946 Nobel Prize in Chemistry for their work. The discovery that enzyme crystals could be grown eventually allowed their actual 3-D structures to be determined by X-ray crystallography. Myoglobin was the first protein to have its structure solved by X-ray crystallography by the British scientists Max Perutz and Sir John Kendrew in 1958. In 1959, Perutz also solved the structure of hemo-globin, which led to the two scientists sharing the 1962 Nobel Prize in Chemistry.

All of these discoveries, especially during the second half of the twentieth century, were due to the development of new techniques, such as gel electro-phoresis, chromatography, **X-ray diffraction**, NMR spectroscopy, and electron microscopy. Combined with new separation and purification methods, these techniques allowed biochemists to discover and study an ever-increasing number of biomolecules. The American biochemist Linus Pauling discovered the helix and sheet structure patterns in proteins and was rewarded with the Nobel Prize in 1954. In 1958, the Cambridge biochemist Fredrick Sanger won the Nobel Prize for discovering protein-sequencing techniques and producing the first protein amino acid sequence, that of insulin.

The new methods also allowed the study of metabolic pathways, such as glycolysis. Perhaps the best known "metabolic" biochemist was the production process for the cell has a high energy cost. This is where photosynthesis could help. Motivated by the efficiency with which plants convert sunlight into sugar, scientists have now started to make solar cells that use photosynthetic proteins to convert light into electricity.

Photosynthesis can also be applied to many more areas than the fabrication of solar cells for energy conversion. For instance,

German-British scientist Hans Krebs, who made important contributions to the study of many metabolic pathways and reaction mechanisms. For the discovery of the Krebs cycle, he won the Nobel Prize in 1953.

The pace of discovery also increased in enzymology, particularly in studies of cellular metabolism. The creation of new substances that could produce other substances made possible the discoveries in DNA and genetic research that followed.

The spectacular discoveries in the area of nucleic acids started with the work of the British scientists Francis Crick, James Watson, and Maurice Wilkins, who were the first to describe the molecular structure of DNA as a double helix made up of two twisted strands. They were jointly awarded the 1962 Nobel Prize for Physiology or Medicine for their discoveries.

Figure 8.3   Linus Pauling also won the Nobel Peace Prize in 1962 for his efforts to end open-air testing of nuclear weapons, making him the only person to win two unshared Nobel Prizes.

photosystems and related molecules could be used in nanotechnology, which involves building devices, such as electronic circuits, from single atoms and molecules. Many chlorophyll-like **pigments** are also used for tumor detection because they tend to accumulate more in tumors cells than in normal cells. Since they are highly fluorescent, they can easily be detected.

The Human
Genome Project

A gene is a unit of DNA that carries the instructions for making a specific protein or set of proteins. The complete set of genes in an organism is its **genome**. The human genome contains some 20,000 to 25,000 genes, and each gene codes for about three proteins. The genes are located on 23 pairs of chromosomes packed into the cell nucleus. They direct the production of proteins with the help of enzymes and messenger molecules such as mRNA. The information in a gene's DNA is copied into mRNA. Then, the mRNA travels out of the nucleus so that its DNA message can be read by small cell structures called **ribosomes**. The ribosomes use the genetic code in the mRNA to link amino acids in a specified order, the first step in making a specific protein.

THE HUMAN GENOME PROJECT

All the cells in the human body contain a complete copy of the approximately 3 billion DNA **base pairs** that make up the human genome. With its four-letter code, DNA contains all the information needed to build the entire human body. Among the first genomes to be mapped were that of the chimpanzee, mouse, rat, pufferfish, fruit fly, roundworm, baker's yeast, and the bacterium *Escherichia coli*. As of 2008, the genomes of some 100 species' genomes are completely known.

The Human Genome Project (HGP) was an international research project with the goals of mapping each human gene and sequencing human DNA. It was directed by the National Institutes of Health (NIH) and the National Human Genome Research Institute. The complete human genome sequence was completed in April 2003 and is now freely available in public databases. The project was an outstanding success and was completed more than two years ahead of schedule.

The DNA sequence used by the Human Genome Project was not that of a single person, but a composite from several individuals; thus it is a representative human sequence. During the project, the identity of the DNA donors was kept anonymous. More blood samples were collected from volunteers than were actually used, and no names were attached to the samples that were analyzed. Thus, not even the donors knew whether their DNA samples were actually used.

GENETIC MAPPING

In additon to sequencing the human genome, the Human Genome Project was also intended to generate new tools and methods that could be used for a broad range of biomedical applications. For instance, new methods were developed for finding genetic changes that increase the risk of specific diseases, such as cancer. Other techniques were invented to look for the type of genetic mutations seen in abnormal cells, such as tumor cells. One of these tools is **genetic mapping**, which locates the positions of specific genes on a chromosome. It is the first step in isolating a gene. Genetic

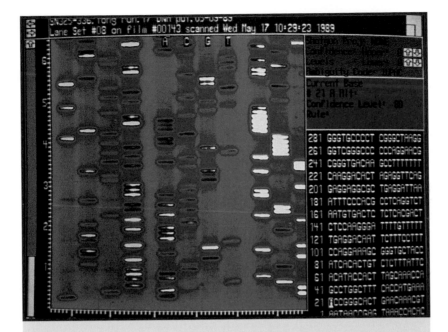

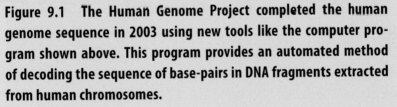

Figure 9.1 The Human Genome Project completed the human genome sequence in 2003 using new tools like the computer program shown above. This program provides an automated method of decoding the sequence of base-pairs in DNA fragments extracted from human chromosomes.

mapping can offer firm evidence that a disease transmitted from parent to child is linked to one or more genes. It also provides clues about which chromosome contains the defective gene and precisely where it is located on that chromosome.

To produce a genetic map, scientists collect blood or tissue samples from family members who have a certain disease. Using various laboratory techniques, they isolate DNA from these samples and examine the pattern of bases seen only in the family members who have the disease. In this way, they can identify the defective gene that causes the disease.

Genetic maps have been used successfully to find the single gene responsible for rare inherited diseases such as **cystic fibrosis** and **muscular dystrophy**. Maps are now being used by scientists to study the genes that are involved in more common diseases, such as asthma, heart disease, diabetes, blindness, and cancer.

DNA SEQUENCING

DNA sequencing simply means figuring out the exact order of the bases in a strand of DNA. In the Human Genome Project, this means the exact order of the 3 billion chemical building blocks that make up the DNA of the human chromosomes. Because the bases pair specifically, biochemists only need to identify the bases in one strand of the double-stranded DNA molecule.

First, chromosomes, which contain from 50 million to 250 million bases, must be extracted from a tissue sample and broken into short pieces. Each piece is then used as a **template** to generate a set of four fragments that differ in length from each other by a single base. Each fragment is also marked with a fluorescent tag that identifies the last base of the fragment. The fragments in a set are separated using a technique called **gel electrophoresis**. This is a method for separating molecules by placing a sample on a gel. An electric current is applied, and the components of the sample separate because some are more charged than others, and therefore migrate faster on the gel. Afterwards, each separate fragment is passed through a detector that reads the fluorescent tag. Then, a computer reconstructs the entire sequence of the long DNA strand by identifying the base at each position from the size of each fragment and the particular fluorescent signal detected at its end.

DNA Microchips

A mutation is a change in the DNA of a specific gene, and it causes a certain disease. However, it is very difficult to detect these mutations, because most large genes have many regions where a mutation can happen. The **DNA microchip** is a new tool being developed to identify mutations. It is simply a chip with artificial DNA for a specific gene on it. To find out whether a person has a mutation in a gene, a scientist first obtains a sample of DNA from the person's blood to compare it to a control sample, namely normal DNA that does not contain a mutation.

The DNA sample is then heated, which unwinds the double helix and separates the two strands of DNA into single-stranded molecules. In the next step, the long strands of DNA are cut into smaller fragments that are marked with a fluorescent dye, just as in sequencing. The person's DNA is labeled with a green dye and the normal DNA with a red dye. Both sets of DNA are then placed into the chip and allowed to bind to the synthetic gene DNA on the chip. If the person does not have a mutation for the gene, both the red and green samples will bind to the sequences on the chip. But if the person has a mutation, the DNA will not bind properly in the region where the mutation is located. The scientist can then confirm that a mutation is present.

Polymerase Chain Reaction

The **polymerase chain reaction** is a technique used to copy small segments of DNA. First, a sample of the desired DNA segment is heated to denature the DNA and separate it into two strands, just like when preparing a DNA microchip. Next, an enzyme called Taq polymerase catalyzes the synthesis of two new strands of DNA, so that each of the original strands is now paired with a new strand. This process results in the duplication of the original DNA, with each of the new molecules containing one old and one new strand of DNA. Then, each of these strands can in turn be used to create two new copies, and so on. The cycle of denaturing and synthesizing new DNA is repeated as many as 50 times, leading to more than one billion exact copies of the original DNA segment. The DNA copies can then be used in many different laboratory procedures, such as the mapping techniques of the Human Genome Project.

GENE TESTING

Gene testing means examining the DNA of a person, usually taken from cells in a sample of blood or from other body fluids or tissues. It is done to look for some change that signals a disease or disorder.

GENE THERAPY

The idea behind **gene therapy** is to treat diseases caused by defective genes by inserting the normal form of the gene into a patient's cells. If gene therapy could work, it could provide a cure for many diseases that are hard to treat.

Patients suffering from hemophilia B may be the first to benefit from gene therapy. Hemophilia is a blood disorder. People who have it tend to bleed strongly at the slightest injury because their blood lacks special proteins called clotting factors that stop bleeding. These clotting factors consist of many proteins that work together to make the blood clot. One of these proteins is called Factor IX, and people who have a defective Factor IX gene suffer from hemophilia B. About 3,300 people in the United States have hemophilia B, and another 12,000 people suffer from hemophilia A, the result of mutations in the gene for Factor VIII, another blood-clotting protein.

Since patients with hemophilia B cannot make Factor IX, they need to inject themselves with it. Researchers recently completed a study involving three patients with hemophilia B. The purpose of the study was simply to test the safety of the gene therapy. From earlier tests in mice and dogs, they had calculated that the amount of the gene given to the patients would be too low to cure the disease. However, to their great surprise, they found that two of the patients actually started improving, and needed fewer injections of Factor IX protein to stop bleeding. Although a safety trial can prove nothing about a treatment's effectiveness, these early results are encouraging because two of the three patients showed a benefit at a very low dose of Factor IX.

The DNA change can be large, such as a missing or added piece of a chromosome that can be seen under a microscope. Or it can be very small, like one extra, missing, or altered nucleotide base.

Genes can also be overexpressed, meaning that too many copies are made, or they can be inactivated or missing altogether. Sometimes, pieces of chromosomes become switched so that a gene ends up in the wrong location. In addition to the examination of chromosomes or genes, genetic testing also includes biochemical tests for the presence or absence of incorrectly made proteins that signal defective genes.

PROTEOMES

Although the genome contains the genetic information of an organism, it is the proteins of which the organism is made that define the organism. Proteins provide the special structure and function that make a particular cell or a tissue type what it is. A **proteome** is the complete set of proteins made by a given cell, tissue, or organism.

Different cells make different proteins, so the proteome of one cell will be different from the proteome of another. In addition, cells that are defective or damaged, such as cancer cells, have a different proteome than normal cells. Therefore, the study of proteomes is an important area of biochemistry because understanding the normal proteome of a cell helps to understand the changes that occur as a result of disease. The study of proteomes, called **proteomics**, seeks to understand the composition, structure, function, and interactions of all the proteins of each living cell.

BIOINFORMATICS

Bioinformatics uses computers to create and maintain large electronic databases on genomes, protein sequences, and proteomes. With the help of protein prediction software, the computer analysis of genome sequences is producing thousands of new proteins of unknown structure and function. These proteins are called hypothetical proteins because they are predicted from the gene sequence. To know if they really exist would require that they be isolated, purified, and subjected to X-ray crystallography or nuclear magnetic resonance (NMR). Therefore, there is no evidence that they are actually made, and there is no known function for them.

Bioinformatics computer programs can at least help determine the structure of proteins whose function is not yet known. This is done by comparing the sequence of the unknown protein to proteins with known three-dimensional structures. The programs can then make a model of the unknown protein's structure by matching its features to that of the known proteins, called *templates*. In addition, when the function of the template protein is known, it can also help identify the function of the unknown protein. These predictive programs cannot produce structures as well as X-ray crystallography or NMR. However, they are very useful in quickly analyzing the large number of new proteins identified by the analysis of whole genomes.

THE FUTURE OF BIOCHEMISTRY

At the start of the twentieth century, biochemistry was dominated by the microbe hunters and replaced later by enzyme and vitamin hunters. In recent decades, biochemistry has been dominated by the gene hunters. The current age of the genome truly represents the most revolutionary advance in the history of biochemistry and medical science. The wealth of information provided by the Human Genome Project lets us anticipate many more exciting discoveries in both genomics and proteomics, areas of study now leading biochemistry in the twenty-first century.

PERIODIC TABLE OF THE ELEMENTS

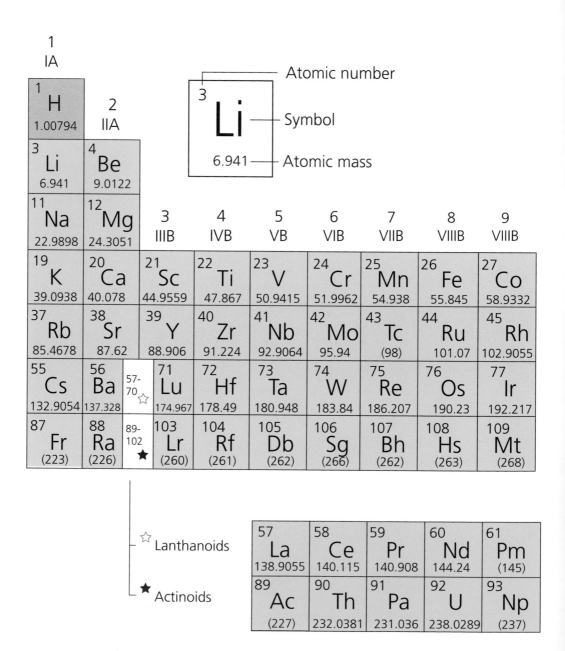

Numbers in parentheses are atomic mass numbers of most stable isotopes.

								18 VIIIA
			13 IIIA	14 IVA	15 VA	16 VIA	17 VIIA	2 He 4.0026
			5 B 10.81	6 C 12.011	7 N 14.0067	8 O 15.9994	9 F 18.9984	10 Ne 20.1798
10 VIIIB	11 IB	12 IIB	13 Al 26.9815	14 Si 28.0855	15 P 30.9738	16 S 32.067	17 Cl 35.4528	18 Ar 39.948
28 Ni 58.6934	29 Cu 63.546	30 Zn 65.409	31 Ga 69.723	32 Ge 72.61	33 As 74.9216	34 Se 78.96	35 Br 79.904	36 Kr 83.798
46 Pd 106.42	47 Ag 107.8682	48 Cd 112.412	49 In 114.818	50 Sn 118.711	51 Sb 121.760	52 Te 127.60	53 I 126.9045	54 Xe 131.29
78 Pt 195.08	79 Au 196.9655	80 Hg 200.59	81 Tl 204.3833	82 Pb 207.2	83 Bi 208.9804	84 Po (209)	85 At (210)	86 Rn (222)
110 Ds (271)	111 Rg (272)	112 Uub (277)	113 Uut (284)	114 Uuq (285)	115 Uup (288)	116 Uuh (292)	117 Uus ?	118 Uuo ?

62 Sm 150.36	63 Eu 151.966	64 Gd 157.25	65 Tb 158.9253	66 Dy 162.500	67 Ho 164.9303	68 Er 167.26	69 Tm 168.9342	70 Yb 173.04
94 Pu (244)	95 Am 243	96 Cm (247)	97 Bk (247)	98 Cf (251)	99 Es (252)	100 Fm (257)	101 Md (258)	102 No (259)

ELECTRON CONFIGURATIONS

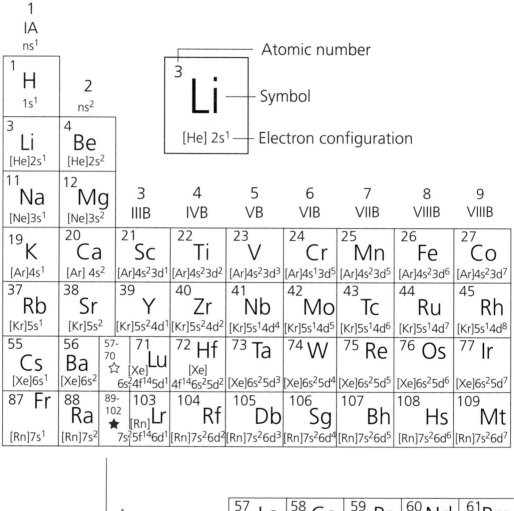

1 IA ns^1								
1 H 1s^1	**2 ns^2**							
3 Li [He]2s^1	**4 Be** [He]2s^2							
11 Na [Ne]3s^1	**12 Mg** [Ne]3s^2	**3 IIIB**	**4 IVB**	**5 VB**	**6 VIB**	**7 VIIB**	**8 VIIIB**	**9 VIIIB**
19 K [Ar]4s^1	**20 Ca** [Ar] 4s^2	**21 Sc** [Ar]4s^{2}3d^1	**22 Ti** [Ar]4s^{2}3d^2	**23 V** [Ar]4s^{2}3d^3	**24 Cr** [Ar]4s^{1}3d^5	**25 Mn** [Ar]4s^{2}3d^5	**26 Fe** [Ar]4s^{2}3d^6	**27 Co** [Ar]4s^{2}3d^7
37 Rb [Kr]5s^1	**38 Sr** [Kr]5s^2	**39 Y** [Kr]5s^{2}4d^1	**40 Zr** [Kr]5s^{2}4d^2	**41 Nb** [Kr]5s^{1}4d^4	**42 Mo** [Kr]5s^{1}4d^5	**43 Tc** [Kr]5s^{1}4d^6	**44 Ru** [Kr]5s^{1}4d^7	**45 Rh** [Kr]5s^{1}4d^8
55 Cs [Xe]6s^1	**56 Ba** [Xe]6s^2	57-70 ☆ **71 Lu** [Xe] 6s^{2}4f^{14}5d^1	**72 Hf** [Xe] 4f^{14}6s^{2}5d^2	**73 Ta** [Xe]6s^{2}5d^3	**74 W** [Xe]6s^{2}5d^4	**75 Re** [Xe]6s^{2}5d^5	**76 Os** [Xe]6s^{2}5d^6	**77 Ir** [Xe]6s^{2}5d^7
87 Fr [Rn]7s^1	**88 Ra** [Rn]7s^2	89-102 ★ **103 Lr** [Rn] 7s^{2}5f^{14}6d^1	**104 Rf** [Rn]7s^{2}6d^2	**105 Db** [Rn]7s^{2}6d^3	**106 Sg** [Rn]7s^{2}6d^4	**107 Bh** [Rn]7s^{2}6d^5	**108 Hs** [Rn]7s^{2}6d^6	**109 Mt** [Rn]7s^{2}6d^7

Atomic number

3 Li [He] 2s^1

Symbol

Electron configuration

☆ Lanthanoids

★ Actinoids

57 La [Xe] 6s^{2}5d^1	**58 Ce** [Xe] 6s^{2}4f^{1}5d^1	**59 Pr** [Xe] 6s^{2}4f^{3}5d^0	**60 Nd** [Xe] 6s^{2}4f^{4}5d^0	**61 Pm** [Xe] 6s^{2}4f^{5}5d^0
89 Ac [Rn]7s^{2}6d^1	**90 Th** [Rn] 7s^{2}5f^{0}6d^2	**91 Pa** [Rn] 7s^{2}5f^{2}6d^1	**92 U** [Rn] 7s^{2}5f^{3}6d^1	**93 Np** [Rn] 7s^{2}5f^{4}6d^1

10 VIIIB	11 IB	12 IIB	13 IIIA ns^2np^1	14 IVA ns^2np^2	15 VA ns^2np^3	16 VIA ns^2np^4	17 VIIA ns^2np^5	18 VIIIA ns^2np^6
								2 He $1s^2$
			5 B [He]$2s^22p^1$	6 C [He]$2s^22p^2$	7 N [He]$2s^22p^3$	8 O [He]$2s^22p^4$	9 F [He]$2s^22p^5$	10 Ne [He]$2s^22p^6$
			13 Al [Ne]$3s^23p^1$	14 Si [Ne]$3s^23p^2$	15 P [Ne]$3s^23p^3$	16 S [Ne]$3s^23p^4$	17 Cl [Ne]$3s^23p^5$	18 Ar [Ne]$3s^23p^6$
28 Ni [Ar]$4s^23d^8$	29 Cu [Ar]$4s^13d^{10}$	30 Zn [Ar]$4s^23d^{10}$	31 Ga [Ar]$4s^24p^1$	32 Ge [Ar]$4s^24p^2$	33 As [Ar]$4s^24p^3$	34 Se [Ar]$4s^24p^4$	35 Br [Ar]$4s^24p^5$	36 Kr [Ar]$4s^24p^6$
46 Pd [Kr]$4d^{10}$	47 Ag [Kr]$5s^14d^{10}$	48 Cd [Kr]$5s^24d^{10}$	49 In [Kr]$5s^25p^1$	50 Sn [Kr]$5s^25p^2$	51 Sb [Kr]$5s^25p^3$	52 Te [Kr]$5s^25p^4$	53 I [Kr]$5s^25p^5$	54 Xe [Kr]$5s^25p^6$
78 Pt [Xe]$6s^15d^9$	79 Au [Xe]$6s^15d^{10}$	80 Hg [Xe]$6s^25d^{10}$	81 Tl [Xe]$6s^26p^1$	82 Pb [Xe]$6s^26p^2$	83 Bi [Xe]$6s^26p^3$	84 Po [Xe]$6s^26p^4$	85 At [Xe]$6s^26p^5$	86 Rn [Xe]$6s^26p^6$
110 Ds [Rn]$7s^16d^9$	111 Rg [Rn]$7s^16d^{10}$	112 Uub [Rn]$7s^26d^{10}$	113 Uut ?	114 Uuq ?	115 Uup ?	116 Uuh ?	117 Uus ?	118 Uuo ?

62 Sm [Xe] $6s^24f^65d^0$	63 Eu [Xe] $6s^24f^75d^0$	64 Gd [Xe] $6s^24f^75d^1$	65 Tb [Xe] $6s^24f^95d^0$	66 Dy [Xe] $6s^24f^{10}5d^0$	67 Ho [Xe] $6s^24f^{11}5d^0$	68 Er [Xe] $6s^24f^{12}5d^0$	69 Tm [Xe] $6s^24f^{13}5d^0$	70 Yb [Xe] $6s^24f^{14}5d^0$
94 Pu [Rn] $7s^25f^66d^0$	95 Am [Rn] $7s^25f^76d^0$	96 Cm [Rn] $7s^25f^76d^1$	97 Bk [Rn] $7s^25f^96d^0$	98 Cf [Rn] $7s^25f^{10}6d^0$	99 Es [Rn] $7s^25f^{11}6d^0$	100 Fm [Rn] $7s^25f^{12}6d^0$	101 Md [Rn] $7s^25f^{13}6d^0$	102 No [Rn] $7s^25f^{14}6d^1$

TABLE OF ATOMIC MASSES

ELEMENT	SYMBOL	ATOMIC NUMBER	ATOMIC MASS	ELEMENT	SYMBOL	ATOMIC NUMBER	ATOMIC MASS
Actinium	Ac	89	(227)	Francium	Fr	87	(223)
Aluminum	Al	13	26.9815	Gadolinium	Gd	64	157.25
Americium	Am	95	243	Gallium	Ga	31	69.723
Antimony	Sb	51	121.76	Germanium	Ge	32	72.61
Argon	Ar	18	39.948	Gold	Au	79	196.9655
Arsenic	As	33	74.9216	Hafnium	Hf	72	178.49
Astatine	At	85	(210)	Hassium	Hs	108	(263)
Barium	Ba	56	137.328	Helium	He	2	4.0026
Berkelium	Bk	97	(247)	Holmium	Ho	67	164.9303
Beryllium	Be	4	9.0122	Hydrogen	H	1	1.00794
Bismuth	Bi	83	208.9804	Indium	In	49	114.818
Bohrium	Bh	107	(262)	Iodine	I	53	126.9045
Boron	B	5	10.81	Iridium	Ir	77	192.217
Bromine	Br	35	79.904	Iron	Fe	26	55.845
Cadmium	Cd	48	112.412	Krypton	Kr	36	83.798
Calcium	Ca	20	40.078	Lanthanum	La	57	138.9055
Californium	Cf	98	(251)	Lawrencium	Lr	103	(260)
Carbon	C	6	12.011	Lead	Pb	82	207.2
Cerium	Ce	58	140.115	Lithium	Li	3	6.941
Cesium	Cs	55	132.9054	Lutetium	Lu	71	174.967
Chlorine	Cl	17	35.4528	Magnesium	Mg	12	24.3051
Chromium	Cr	24	51.9962	Manganese	Mn	25	54.938
Cobalt	Co	27	58.9332	Meitnerium	Mt	109	(268)
Copper	Cu	29	63.546	Mendelevium	Md	101	(258)
Curium	Cm	96	(247)	Mercury	Hg	80	200.59
Darmstadtium	Ds	110	(271)	Molybdenum	Mo	42	95.94
Dubnium	Db	105	(262)	Neodymium	Nd	60	144.24
Dysprosium	Dy	66	162.5	Neon	Ne	10	20.1798
Einsteinium	Es	99	(252)	Neptunium	Np	93	(237)
Erbium	Er	68	167.26	Nickel	Ni	28	58.6934
Europium	Eu	63	151.966	Niobium	Nb	41	92.9064
Fermium	Fm	100	(257)	Nitrogen	N	7	14.0067
Fluorine	F	9	18.9984	Nobelium	No	102	(259)

ELEMENT	SYMBOL	ATOMIC NUMBER	ATOMIC MASS
Osmium	Os	76	190.23
Oxygen	O	8	15.9994
Palladium	Pd	46	106.42
Phosphorus	P	15	30.9738
Platinum	Pt	78	195.08
Plutonium	Pu	94	(244)
Polonium	Po	84	(209)
Potassium	K	19	39.0938
Praseodymium	Pr	59	140.908
Promethium	Pm	61	(145)
Protactinium	Pa	91	231.036
Radium	Ra	88	(226)
Radon	Rn	86	(222)
Rhenium	Re	75	186.207
Rhodium	Rh	45	102.9055
Roentgenium	Rg	111	(272)
Rubidium	Rb	37	85.4678
Ruthenium	Ru	44	101.07
Rutherfordium	Rf	104	(261)
Samarium	Sm	62	150.36
Scandium	Sc	21	44.9559
Seaborgium	Sg	106	(266)
Selenium	Se	34	78.96

ELEMENT	SYMBOL	ATOMIC NUMBER	ATOMIC MASS
Silicon	Si	14	28.0855
Silver	Ag	47	107.8682
Sodium	Na	11	22.9898
Strontium	Sr	38	87.62
Sulfur	S	16	32.067
Tantalum	Ta	73	180.948
Technetium	Tc	43	(98)
Tellurium	Te	52	127.6
Terbium	Tb	65	158.9253
Thallium	Tl	81	204.3833
Thorium	Th	90	232.0381
Thulium	Tm	69	168.9342
Tin	Sn	50	118.711
Titanium	Ti	22	47.867
Tungsten	W	74	183.84
Ununbium	Uub	112	(277)
Uranium	U	92	238.0289
Vanadium	V	23	50.9415
Xenon	Xe	54	131.29
Ytterbium	Yb	70	173.04
Yttrium	Y	39	88.906
Zinc	Zn	30	65.409
Zirconium	Zr	40	91.224

GLOSSARY

Acids **Hydrocarbons** with a hydrogen replaced by a carboxyl (COOH) group. In solution, acids can release a hydrogen ion: $COOH \rightarrow COO- + H^+$.

Active site The region on an enzyme that binds the substrate.

Aerobic In the presence of oxygen.

Alcohol Hydrocarbon with a hydrogen replaced by an OH group.

Amine Hydrocarbon with a hydrogen replaced by a NH_2 group. It is basic, because it can accept hydrogen ions: $NH_2 + H^+ \rightarrow NH_{3+}$.

Amino acids Molecules with carboxyl and amino groups; the building blocks of proteins.

Amino group A functional group with one nitrogen and two hydrogen atoms: NH_2.

Anabolism Metabolic pathways that require energy and produce larger, more complex molecules from smaller ones—for example, the production of proteins from amino acids.

Anaerobic In the absence of oxygen.

ATP Adenosine triphosphate, a high-energy molecule used to fuel chemical reactions in cells.

Atom The smallest component of an element that has the properties of the element. Atoms consist of a nucleus of positive protons and neutral neutrons surrounded by negative electrons.

Bacteria Single-celled microorganisms that live in soil, water, organic matter, or the bodies of plants and animals. Many cause disease.

Base Nitrogen-containing compounds that are parts of the nucleotides that make up nucleic acids. The most common bases are adenine (A), cytosine (C), guanine (G), thymine (T) and uracil (U).

Base pair In a nucleic acid, two bases on different strands that interact by hydrogen bonding; in DNA, G pairs with C and A pairs with T, while in RNA, G pairs with C and A pairs with U.

Biochemistry   The study of all molecules synthesized by and used by living organisms.

Bioinformatics   The use of computers in the life sciences. Bioinformatics is used to create extensive electronic databases on genomes and protein sequences. It is also used to model the 3D structure of unknown biomolecules.

Biomolecule   Any molecule used or made by a living organism.

Biosensor   A device that detects a particular chemical in a biological sample.

Biotechnology   Any technology that uses living organisms, or parts of organisms, to make or modify products.

Bond   A chemical bond is created when two atoms share or donate electrons to each other. They can be single, double, or triple, involving one, two, or three pairs of electrons, respectively.

Calorie   A unit of scientific measure for heat and energy. One calorie is the amount of energy needed to raise the temperature of one gram of water by one degree Celsius.

Carbohydrates   Biochemical compounds composed of carbon, hydrogen, and oxygen; include sugars, starch, cellulose, and glycogen.

Carbon   Element that has the symbol C. It is found in rocks and in all living organisms. It is also the major component of graphite, charcoal, and diamonds.

Carboxyl group   Chemical functional group with one carbon, one hydrogen, and two oxygen atoms: COOH. It is an acid group because it can release a hydrogen ion.

Catabolism   Metabolic pathways that degrade molecules and complex compounds into smaller, simpler ones, releasing energy in the process.

Catalyst   A substance that can increase the rate of a chemical reaction.

Cell   The basic structural unit of living organisms; the smallest unit capable of independent life.

Cell membrane   Semipermeable layer enclosing all the components of a cell. It is made of a lipid bilayer that contains protein channels to let substances in and out.

Cell wall   In plants, the rigid cellulose structure that surrounds the membrane of a cell. In bacteria, the outer layer exposed to the environment.

Cellular respiration   The process by which all living cells produce energy.

Cellulose   A polysaccharide found in plants, consisting of long chains of glucose molecules. It maintains the structure of the cell walls and protects and strengthens the plant. Cellulose is the most abundant compound on earth made by living organisms.

Chemical Formula   A scientific notation that identifies the number of atoms in one molecule of a compound. It is written with element symbols and the numbers of atoms in subscript. The formula for carbon dioxide is CO_2. One molecule contains one carbon atom and two oxygen atoms.

Chitin   A carbohydrate found in the shells of crustaceans such as lobsters and crabs and that provides support and protection.

Chlorophyll   Green pigment that can absorb light rays during photosynthesis. It captures the energy from the sun and transforms it into chemical bond energy. Chlorophylls are found in the chloroplasts of plants and algae and in some bacteria.

Chloroplast   The structure in the cells of green plants and algae in which photosynthesis takes place.

Cholesterol   A lipid steroid found in animal tissue and fat.

Chromatin   The complex of DNA and associated proteins found in the nucleus of cells.

Chromosomes   Structures in a cell nucleus that contain the genes and their genetic information. They occur in pairs, one from the mother and one from the father.

Concentration   The amount of one substance in a system relative to the amount of other substances.

Covalent bond   A chemical bond where electrons are shared between two atoms.

Cristae   Tightly folded inner membranes of mitochondria where ATP is made.

Cystic fibrosis   A rare genetic disease affecting the lining of the lungs, leading to breathing problems and other difficulties.

Cytoplasm   The substance that fills the cell between the nucleus and the cell membrane; it contains many microscopic structures.

Digestion   The process of breaking down food into its constituent chemical substances.

Disaccharide   A carbohydrate made up of two monosaccharides (simple sugars).

Disulfide bond   Bonds that form in the tertiary structure of proteins between two sulfur atoms of cysteine amino acids in the polypeptide chains.

DNA   Deoxyribonucleic acid. The nucleic acid that carries the genetic information of an organism. It is the primary component of chromosomes.

DNA microchip   Chip coated with the DNA of a gene; used to look for gene mutations.

DNA sequencing   Identification of the exact order of the bases in a strand of DNA.

Effector   Substance that facilitates a process or reaction.

Electron   Atomic particle with a charge of -1; found in the space around the nucleus of an atom.

Electron transport chain   A series of reactions that takes place within the mitochondria that result in the production of ATP. It is a major process of aerobic respiration.

Electronegative   Molecules or atoms that attract electrons to form a chemical bond.

Element   A substance made of one kind of atom that cannot be broken down by ordinary physical means.

Enzymes   Proteins that control and speed up biochemical reactions.

Ethanol   Alcohol made by converting carbohydrates to sugar, which is then converted to ethanol by fermentation. Formula: CH_3-CH_2-OH.

Fat-soluble   Any molecule that can dissolve in fats, such as vitamins A, D, E, and K.

Fatty acid   A molecule with a carboxylic acid on a long chain of carbon atoms. Fatty acids are a major source of energy for the cell. They are also used to make phospholipids.

Fermentation   Chemical conversion of sugar to alcohol or acids by the action of yeast or some kinds of bacteria or by muscle cells.

Gel electrophoresis   Biochemical separation technique that separates the components of a mixture using a gel in which the components migrate at different speeds depending on their charge.

Gene   Ordered sequence of nucleotides located in a particular position on a particular chromosome and containing instructions to make a specific product, such as a protein molecule. Genes are the fundamental units of heredity.

Gene therapy   Insertion of normal DNA directly into cells to correct a defective gene.

Genetic mapping   The process of locating the positions of specific genes on a chromosome.

Genome The complete set of genetic information of a living organism.

Glucose Simple sugar with formula $C_6H_{12}O_6$. It is the primary chemical product of photosynthesis and the component of starch, glycogen, and cellulose.

Glycerol A three-carbon molecule with three alcohol functional groups. It is the basic molecule that combines with fatty acids to make fat molecules.

Glycogen Storage form of glucose in animals and humans.

Glycolysis A metabolic pathway of living cells with the sequence of enzyme reactions that converts glucose into lactic acid (anaerobic glycolysis) or into pyruvate (aerobic glycolysis).

Granum (pl. grana) A closely packed stack of thylakoid membranes in a chloroplast.

Hemoglobin Protein found in the blood that binds oxygen molecules and transports them to the cells of the body.

Heparin Complex polysaccharide used as a drug to prevent blood clotting.

Hormone A chemical substance produced in the body that controls the activity of certain cells or organs.

Hydrocarbon Molecules that contain only carbon and hydrogen.

Hydrogen Element that has the symbol H. It is the first element in the periodic table. It is also the smallest atom. There is more hydrogen in the universe than any other element.

Hydrogen bond A weak chemical bond that has hydrogen bonded to an electronegative atom, often oxygen.

Hydronium ion Positive ion resulting from the ionization of water: $2H_2O \rightarrow H_3O^+ + OH^-$

Hydrophilic Compounds that are water loving. Hydrophilic compounds dissolve easily in water and are usually polar.

Hydrophobic   Compounds that are water fearing. Hydrophobic compounds do not dissolve easily in water and are usually non-polar. Oils and other long hydrocarbons are hydrophobic.

Hydroxide ion   A negatively charged ion that has one hydrogen atom bonded to one oxygen atom: OH-

Immunoglobulins   Proteins that are antibodies, which fight disease and destroy foreign invaders.

Inhibitor   Substance that prevents or slows down the activity of a process.

Insoluble   A substance that cannot dissolve in another substance.

Ion   A small molecule or atom that has a positive or negative charge. A molecule or chemical group that can be changed into an ion is referred to as *ionizable*. For example, the COOH group can ionize to COO^-, an ion with a negative charge. The splitting of molecules into negatively and positively charged ions is called *ionization*.

Krebs cycle   The second metabolic pathway in aerobic cell respiration; converts carbohydrates and lipids (sugars and fats) into carbon dioxide and water and produces energy-rich compounds, including some ATP.

Lipid bilayer   Ordered double layer of phospholipid molecules arranged so that the hydrophilic heads (phosphate groups) are on the outside and the hydrophobic tails (fatty-acid chains) are on the inside facing each other.

Lipids   A class of biochemical compounds that includes fats, oils, and waxes.

Metabolic pathway   A series of biochemical reactions catalyzed by enzymes in a living organism.

Metabolism   All the biochemical processes that occur in living cells or organisms and that are necessary for the maintenance of life.

Mitochondrion (pl. mitochondria) Part of the cell where ATP is made. It also contains genetic material.

Molecule A group of atoms bonded together. The atoms can be different, as in water, H_2O, or the same, as in ozone, O_3.

Monomeric protein Protein that has only one amino acid chain.

Monosaccharide A simple sugar, such as glucose. It usually has 6 carbon, 12 hydrogen, and 6 oxygen atoms with the formula $(CH_2O)x$, where x can be any number of repeating CH_2O units.

Multimeric Protein that consists of many monomers.

Muscular dystrophy A rare genetic disease of the muscles. It causes the muscles in the body to become very weak. They break down and are replaced with fatty deposits over time.

Mutation Change in the DNA sequence of a gene to some new form.

Myoglobin Protein that stores oxygen in muscle cells.

NADH Nicotinamide adenine dinucleotide. A molecule that carries energy.

Nitrogen Element that has the symbol N. It is found as a gas in nature and makes up almost 80% of the air. It is also found in the soil and is a major nutrient for plants.

Nonpolar Molecule that has an even distribution of positive and negative charges and is not soluble in water.

Nucleic acids A class of biochemical compounds that includes DNA and RNA.

Nucleotide Unit from which nucleic acids are made. It contains a sugar, a phosphate group, and a nitrogen base.

Nucleus The nucleus of an atom is the positively charged portion of the atom that contains protons and neutrons. Negatively charged electrons are found in the space around the nucleus. The nucleus of a cell, which is surrounded by a membrane, contains the chromosomes with their DNA and hereditary information.

Oxidation   A chemical reaction in which an atom loses one or more electrons.

Oxygen   Element that has the symbol O. A reactive gas found in the crust of the Earth and in the air. Most living organisms need oxygen to survive.

Pectin   Polysaccharide found in fruits and vegetables and used to cause various foods to jell.

Peptide   Two or more amino acids joined together.

Peptide bond   The —CO—NH—bond formed between the carboxyl group of one amino acid and the amino group of another.

pH   A measure of the acidity of a substance. A pH less than 7 indicates an acid. A pH of 7 indicates a neutral solution, and a pH above 7 indicates a base.

Phosphate group   An ion consisting of a phosphorus atom and four oxygen atoms: PO_4. Also called inorganic phosphate (Pi).

Phospholipids   Lipids that contain a phosphate group and long fatty-acid chains. They make up cell membranes.

Photosynthesis   Biochemical process in which light energy is absorbed by chlorophyll and used to fuel the building of sugar molecules.

Photosystem   Large protein assembly containing the chlorophyll that captures light during photosynthesis. There are two photosystems, I and II, both located in the chloroplasts of leaves.

Pigment   Any colorful molecule; chlorophyll is the dominant pigment in most plants.

Polar   Molecule that has a pair of equal and opposite charges. It dissolves well in water because water is also polar.

Polarity   The tendency of a molecule to have positive and negative regions because of the unequal sharing of a pair of electrons.

Polymerase chain reaction   Fast technique used to copy DNA.

Polypeptide   Long chain of amino acids joined together.

Polysaccharide   Long chain of sugar molecules. The chain can include many different monosaccharides.

Porphyrin   Large ring of carbons that contains four central nitrogens linked to a metal ion. In hemoglobin, the metal ion is iron; in chlorophylls, it is magnesium.

Preservative   A substance that can prevent the growth of microorganisms.

Primary structure   The linear sequence of amino acids that make up a protein.

Prion   A small protein molecule that has no DNA or RNA. Prions are believed to cause Creutzfeldt-Jakob disease, also known as Mad Cow disease.

Protein   A class of biomolecules constructed from amino acids. Proteins may be structural, like those that make up hair and cartilage, or they may be enzymes that control biochemical reactions.

Protein sequencing   Identification of the consecutive arrangement of all the amino acids that make up a protein.

Proteome   The complete set of proteins made by a cell, tissue, or organism.

Proteomics   The study of proteins and their functions.

Proton   Particle in the nucleus of an atom with a charge of +1.

Quaternary structure   The structure formed by the association of two or more peptide chains.

Ribosome   Site of protein synthesis in a cell.

RNA   Ribonucleic acid. The nucleic acid that carries the information in DNA out of the nucleus to the structures in the cell cytoplasm, where it is interpreted and used.

Saccharide   Scientific name for sugar.

Saturated fat   A type of fat whose fatty-acid chains have no double or triple bonds and cannot accept any more hydrogen atoms.

Secondary structure   The protein structure characterized by folding of the peptide chain into a helix, sheet, or random coil.

Semipermeable   A membrane that allows some, but not all, substances to pass through it.

Soluble   A substance that can dissolve in another substance. Sugar and salt are compounds that are soluble in water.

Starch   A polysaccharide made of glucose units made in plants and used as an energy source.

Steroid   Lipid molecule that has three 6-carbon rings, one 5-carbon ring, and a side chain of some type. They often function as hormones.

Stoma   (pl. stomata) Small pores in plant leaves or stems through which gases can pass.

Structural formula   A chemical formula that shows how atoms are arranged in a molecule and how they are bonded.

Substrate   Molecules acted upon by enzymes. They bind to the enzyme's active site to create an enzyme-substrate complex.

Sugar   Any of several carbohydrates, such as glucose, that are sweet to the taste.

Synthesis   Creation of a new compound from different chemical molecules.

Template   A cut-out pattern or shape used to trace a design, like a stencil. Also, a molecule that serves as a pattern for the creation of another macromolecule.

Tertiary structure   The complete three-dimensional structure of a protein.

Thylakoids   Stack of membranes located in the chloroplasts of plant cells. They contain the chlorophyll molecules that capture light during photosynthesis.

Toxic   Capable of causing injury or damage to a living organism.

Triglyceride   Fat molecule consisting of a molecule of glycerol bonded to three fatty acids.

Unsaturated fat   A type of fat in which the fatty-acid chains have one or more carbon-carbon double bonds and that can accept hydrogen atoms.

Urea   A waste product of the metabolism of proteins that is formed by the liver and eliminated from the body through the kidneys as urine.

Vacuum   Empty space that that has no pressure and no molecules in it.

Virus   A tiny particle that can only multiply within cells. It consists of a strand of either DNA or RNA, but not both, in a protein covering called a capsid.

Waxes   Lipids with long carbon chains that function in nature as protective coatings.

X-ray diffraction   The scattering of X-rays by crystal atoms, producing a diffraction pattern that yields information about the structure of the crystal.

BIBLIOGRAPHY

Berg, J.M., J.L. Tymoczko, and L. Stryer. *Biochemistry*. 6th ed. New York: W.H. Freeman, 2007.

Blankenship, R.E. *Molecular Mechanisms of Photosynthesis*. Oxford: Blackwell Publishing Limited, 2002.

Boyer, R. *Interactive Concepts in Biochemistry*. 2nd ed. New York: John Wiley & Sons, 2002.

Chen, S. "Length of a Human DNA Molecule," The Physics Factbook Web site. Available online. URL: http://hypertextbook.com/facts.

Fickert, P., T. Moustafa, and M. Trauner. "Primary sclerosing cholangitis—The arteriosclerosis of the bile duct?" *Lipids in Health and Disease 6(2007)*: 1–8.

Gilbert, H.F. *Basic Concepts in Biochemistry—A Student's Survival Guide*. 2nd ed. New York: McGraw-Hill, 2000.

Goodsell, D.S. "Photosystem II." *RCSB Molecule of the Month* (November 2004): Available online. URL: http://www.resb.org.

Kornberg, A. "Centenary of the birth of modern biochemistry." *FASEB* 11(1997): 1209–1214.

Loney, D. "Waxing Scientific: Friction and Ski Wax." American Chemical Society Web site. Available online. URL: http://www.chemistry.org/portal/a/c/s/1/feature_ent.html?id=0f1f9724224411d6eac36ed9fe800100.

Murray, R.K., D.K. Granner, P.A. Mayes, and V.W. Rodwell, *Harper's Illustrated Biochemistry*. 27th ed. New York: McGraw-Hill Medical, 2006.

Nelson, D.L., and M.M. Cox. *Lehninger Principles of Biochemistry*, 4th ed. New York: W.H. Freeman, 2004.

Stenesh, J. *Dictionary of Biochemistry and Molecular Biology*. 2nd ed. New York: John Wiley & Sons, 1989.

FURTHER READING

Bankston, J. *Francis Crick and James Watson: Pioneers in DNA Research.* Hockessin, Del.: Mitchell Lane Publishers, 2002.

Branden, C.I. *Introduction to Protein Structure.* 2nd ed. Oxford: Routledge, 1999.

Campbell, A.M., and L.J. Heyer. *Discovering Genomics, Proteomics and Bioinformatics.* 2nd ed. Boston: Benjamin Cummings, 2005.

Debré, P., and E. Forster. *Louis Pasteur.* Baltimore: The Johns Hopkins University Press, 2006.

Fruton, J.S. *Proteins, Enzymes, Genes: The Interplay of Chemistry and Biology.* New Haven: Yale University Press, 1999.

Hume, D., and A. Bechamp. *The Mystery of Fermentation.* Whitefish, Mont.: Kessinger Publishing LLC, 2005.

Kalman, B. *Photosynthesis: Changing Sunlight Into Food.* New York: Crabtree Publishing Company, 2005.

Koolman, J., and K.H. Röhm. *Color Atlas of Biochemistry.* 2nd ed. New York: Thieme Medical Publishers, 2004.

Kornberg, A. *For the Love of Enzymes: The Odyssey of a Biochemist.* Cambridge: Harvard University Press, 1991.

Nelson, D.L., and M.M. Cox. *Lehninger Principles of Biochemistry.* 4th ed. New York: W.H. Freeman, 2004.

Palladino, M.A. *Understanding the Human Genome Project.* 2nd ed. Boston: Benjamin Cummings, 2005.

Tanford, C., and J. Reynolds. *Nature's Robots: A History of Proteins.* New York, NY: Oxford University Press, 2003.

Watson, J.D. *The Double Helix: A Personal Account of the Discovery of the Structure of DNA.* New York: 1st Touchstone ed., 2001.

Wolfe, S.L. *Introduction to Cell Biology.* Emeryville, Calif.: Wadsworth Publishing Company, 1999.

Web Sites

Amino Acids

http://www.biology.arizona.edu/biochemistry/problem_sets/aa/
   Anim/Gly_Leu.html

Animation that shows the structural similarities between the different amino acids.

Basic Chemistry for Understanding Biology

http://www.biology.arizona.edu/biochemistry/tutorials/chemistry/
   page1.html

This web site provides a review of the basic chemistry of small molecules. It explains how electrons determine the properties of elements, the interplay of chemical bonds and attractive forces, and the chemistry of water and simple organic molecules.

Beginner's Guide to Molecular Biology

http://www.rothamsted.ac.uk/notebook/courses/guide/

This resource is maintained by the Molecular Biology Notebook Online project. It provides a wealth of information on the most important aspects of molecular biology such as life, structure and components of the cell, chromosome and DNA structure, protein structure, and diversity.

Biochemistry Online

http://employees.csbsju.edu/hjakubowski/classes/ch331/bcintro/
   default.html

This website provides a comprehensive introduction to biochemistry with a collection of molecular biology/biochemistry online dictionaries, textbooks, and learning modules.

Chemistry of Amino Acids

http://www.med.unibs.it/~marchesi/aacids.html

This resource describes the classification and chemistry of amino acids, covering the α-amino acids of proteins and their acid-base properties, the functional significance of R groups, and the peptide bond.

The Chemistry of Water

http://www.nsf.gov/news/special_reports/water/index.jsp

National Science Foundation website dedicated to the unique and mysterious properties of water.

http://witcombe.sbc.edu/water/chemistrystructure.html

Another website that explains the strange chemistry of water.

Genomes Online Database

http://www.genomesonline.org/

Web resource that provides access to information about completed and ongoing genome projects around the world.

High School Chemistry on the Web

The Chem Team

http://dbhs.wvusd.k12.ca.us/webdocs/ChemTeamIndex.html

A complete tutorial covering all standard topics for students in high school chemistry with several links to chemistry resources.

Basic Chemistry Concepts

http://staff.jccc.net/pdecell/chemistry/chemtext.html

This website describes the basic chemistry concepts required to understand biology, from the periodic table to the types of chemical bonds and molecular interactions. A biochemical gallery of the most important organic molecules for life is also included.

Interactive Metabolic Pathways

http://ull.chemistry.uakron.edu/Pathways/index.html

Website that describes the major metabolic pathways and their reactions.

List of Basic Biochemistry Topics

http://en.wikipedia.org/wiki/List_of_basic_biochemistry_topics

Wikipedia article that provides links to important biochemistry topics such as the major categories of bio-compounds, chemical properties, structural compounds in cells, animals and plants, enzymes, biological membranes, and energy pathways.

The Main Metabolic Pathways on Internet
http://home.wxs.nl/~pvsanten/mmp/mmp.html

Another resource describing the major metabolic pathways.

National Human Genome Research Institute
http://www.genome.gov

Official website of the National Human Genome Research Institute (NHGRI), established in 1989 to carry out the role of the National Institutes of Health (NIH) in the International Human Genome Project (HGP). NHGRI is now one of 27 institutes and centers that make up the NIH.

Photosynthesis
http://www.emc.maricopa.edu/faculty/farabee/BIOBK/BioBookPS.html

This website provides an overview of photosynthesis, including leaf structure, the nature of light, chlorophyll and accessory pigments, chloroplast, and stages of photosynthesis. Several links to other photosynthesis resources are also provided.

PHOTO CREDITS

INDEX

A

absorption, 69
acetylcholinesterase, 38
acid lipase disease, 63
acids, 12. *See also* pH
actin, 23, 24
active sites, 31–32, 34
adenine, 24–28
adenosine diphosphate (ADP), 58
adenosine triphosphate (ATP),
   38–39, 56–58, 60, 68
ADP (adenosine diphosphate), 58
aerobic respiration, 59–60
alanine, 11
albumin, 24
alcohol dehydrogenase, 36
algae, 65
alpha (α) helix structure,
   19–20, 70
amine groups, 9, 12, 19
amino acids
   digestion and, 55
   overview of, 9–12, 15
   protein structure and, 2,
     17–19
   table of, 11
ammonia, 61
amylase, 56
amylose, 50
anabolic steroids, 46
anabolism, 55
anaerobic respiration, 60
antibiotics, 35–36
antibodies, 22, 24
arginine, 11
ascorbic acid, 7
asparagine, 11
aspartic acid, 11
atherosclerosis, 6
ATP, 38–39, 56–58, 60, 68
ATP synthase, 38–39

B

backbones, 15
bacteria, 35–36, 51, 52, 59
bacteriochlorophyll, 65–66
beer, 52
beta (β) sheet structure, 19–20, 70
bioinformatics, 79–80
biomolecules, overview of, 2–5
biotechnology, 37, 68–72
blood clotting, 24
bread, 52
Büchner, Eduard, 62
B vitamins, 46

C

calcium pump protein, 17
carbohydrates
   cellulose as, 50–51
   digestion and, 56
   examples of, 53
   fermentation and, 52
   glycogen as, 51–52
   monosaccharides as, 49
   overview of, 2, 48–49
   polysaccharides as, 49
   starch as, 50
carbon, 9, 10, 52
carbonation, 52
carbon dioxide, 52, 60, 65, 68
carbonyl groups, 11, 15
carboxyl groups, 9, 19
carotenoids, 67
catabolism, 54, 55
catalysts, 33, 34
cell culture techniques, 4
cell membranes, 3–5, 13, 42
cellular respiration, 58–60
cellulose, 2, 49, 50–51, 52
cell walls, 51
centrifugation, 4
charge, enzyme activity and, 32
chemical formulas, 9–12
chemical reactions, 33
chemical symbols, 10
chewing, 56
chitin, 53
chlorophyll, 65–66
chloroplasts, 65–68
cholesterol, 44–45, 47
chromatin, 26, 28–29

chromatography, 4, 70
chromophores, 66
chromosomes, 28–29, 73, 76
chyme, 58
cilia, 23
clotting, 24
clotting factors, 78
collagen, 24
constructive metabolism, 55
cooking, vitamins and, 46
covalent bonds, 12
Crick, Francis, 71
cristae, 56, 57
crystallization, 70
cysteine, 11, 21
cystic fibrosis, 75
cytochrome c, 16, 19
cytochromes, 16, 19, 24
cytoplasm, 56–57
cytosine, 24–28

D
destructive metabolism, 54, 55
diabetes, 7–8, 37
digestion, 55–58
diseases, 5–8, 37, 61–63, 75
disulfide bridges, 21
DNA
    bioinformatics and, 79–80
    discovery of structure of, 71
    genes and, 73
    gene testing and, 77–79
    genetic mapping and, 74–76
    genomes and, 74
    microchips and, 76–77
    mitochondria and, 56–57
    overview of, 2, 26–29
    PCR and, 77
    sequencing of, 74, 76
DNA microchips, 76–77
DNA polymerase, 5
double helix shape of DNA, 27

E
effectors, 34
electrical charges, 13

electromagnetic spectrum, 66–67
electronegativity, 13
electron microscopy, 70
electrons, 12, 16, 56–57, 68
electron transport chain, 59–60
electrophoresis, 4, 70, 76
elements, 10
energy. *See also* Metabolism;
    Photosynthesis
    ATP synthase and, 38–39
    carbohydrates and, 48–49,
        51–52
    fats and, 40, 42
    fatty acids and, 23
    mitochondria and, 56–57
enzymes. *See also Specific enzymes*
    crystallization of, 70
    digestion and, 56–58
    discovery of, 62
    diseases and, 37, 61–63
    factors controlling activity of,
        33–34
    mechanism of action of, 31–33
    metabolism and, 55, 60–63
    as proteins, 2
enzyme specificity, 34
enzyme-substrate (ES)
    complexes, 32
enzymology, 2–4, 71
estradiol, 46
ethanol, 52, 60
eukaryotes, 3

F
Factor IX, 78
$FADH_2$, 60
fats, 2, 40–42
fatty acids, 8, 23, 36, 55, 61
feathers, 43
fermentation, 52, 60, 62
fibrin, 17
fibrinogen, 24
fibrous protein structure, 22
flagella, 23
Fleming, Alexander, 35–36
food delivery, 23

G

gateways, examples of, 24
gel electrophoresis, 4, 70, 76
genes, 5–8, 73. *See also* DNA
gene therapy, 78
genetic mapping, 74–76
genomes, 73, 74
globular protein structure, 22
gluconeogenesis, 61
glucose
    ATP and, 58
    digestion and, 55
    glycogen and, 51–52
    as monosaccharide, 48–50
    photosynthesis and, 65
    respiration and, 60
glucose oxidase, 37
glutamic acid, 11, 21
glutamine, 11
glutamine synthetase, 17
glycerol, 40–41
glycine, 11
glycogen, 48–49, 51–52
glycolysis, 59–60, 70–71
glycoproteins, 24
grains, 52
grana, 65, 67
guanine, 24–28

H

hemes, 61
hemoglobin
    function of, 22
    porphyrins and, 61, 63
    sickle-cell anemia and, 5–6
    structure of, 21, 70
    as transport protein, 24
hemophilia, 78
hemp, 51
heparin, 53
heredity, 5
hexuronic acid, 7
histidine, 11
hops, 52
hormones, 19, 24, 44–46

Human Genome Project (HGP), 74–80
hydrogen, 9, 10, 12–14, 68
hydrogen (H) bonds
    lipid bilayers and, 44
    nucleic acids and, 27
    protein secondary structure and, 19
    protein tertiary structure and, 20–21
    water and, 13, 14
hydrogen ions, 12
hydrogen peroxide, 37
hydronium ions, 14
hydrophilic, 13
hydrophobic, 13
hydroxide ions, 14

I

ice, hydrogen bonds and, 13
immunoglobulins, 22, 24
inhibitors, 34
insulin, 19, 24, 70
ionic bonds, 20
ion pumps, 38–39
ions, 14
iron, oxidation of, 10
isoleucine, 11

K

Kendrew, John, 70
keratin, 24
kinetic experiments, 4
Krebs, Hans, 71
Krebs cycle, 56, 59–60, 71
Kühne, Wilhelm, 62

L

lactic acid, 59
length of DNA in genome, 28
light, 66–67, 69
Limeys, 7
Lind, James, 7
linen, 51
lipid bilayers, 42, 44

lipids
    atherosclerosis and, 6
    digestion and, 56
    fats as, 40–42
    overview of, 2
    phospholipids, 42
    steroids as, 44–46
    vitamins and, 46–47
    waxes as, 42–44
"lock and key" hypothesis,
    31–32
lubrication, 24
lysine, 11
lysozyme, 35–36

M
malt, 52
mapping, genetic, 74–76
matrix, 56–57
medicine, 5–8, 37, 61–63, 75
membranes
    cellular, 3–5, 13, 42
    chloroplasts and, 65, 68
    mitochondria and, 56–57
    nuclear, 3
    phospholipids and, 42
    thylakoid, 65, 67
messenger RNA (mRNA), 30, 73
metabolic pathways, 8
metabolism
    ATP and, 58
    cellular respiration and,
        58–60
    digestion and, 55–58
    disorders of, 61–63
    enzymology and, 3
    other pathways of, 61
    overview of, 54–55
methionine, 11
microchips, DNA, 76–77
microscopy, 4
microtubules, 23
mitochondria, 56–57, 60
molecular modeling, 4
monomeric proteins, 21

monosaccharides, 48, 49
movement, 24
multimeric proteins, 16
muscular dystrophy, 75
mutations, 5–6, 76–77
myoglobin, 24, 61, 70
myosin, 16, 24

N
NADH, 60
NADPH, 68
National Human Genome
    Institute, 74
National Institutes of Health
    (NIH), 74
nervous system, 38
Neuberg, C.A., 62
neurotransmitters, 38
nitrogen, 9, 10
NMR spectroscopy, 70, 80
Northrop, John H., 70
nuclear magnetic resonance
    (NMR), 4
nuclear membranes, 3
nuclei, 26
nucleic acids. *See also* DNA
    discovery of structure of, 71
    medicine, biochemistry and,
        5–8
    overview of, 2, 24–26
    RNA, 2, 29
    RNA polymerase and, 36–38
nucleotides, 24–25
nutrients, delivery of to cells, 23

O
oils, 2, 40–41
organelles, 3
oxidation, 10, 61
oxygen
    amino acids and, 9
    cellular respiration and, 58–60
    overview of, 10
    photosynthesis and, 65, 68
    water and, 12–14

P

paper industry, 51
particle, light as, 69
Pasteur, Louis, 62
Pauling, Linus, 70, 71
PCR (polymerase chain
   reaction), 77
pectin, 53
peptide bonds, 15, 17–19
peptides, 9
permeability, 42
Perutz, Max, 70
pH, 14, 32, 33–34
phenylalanine, 11
phenylalanine hydroxylase, 61, 63
phenylketonuria, 61, 63
phosphate groups, 58
phospholipid bilayers, 42, 44
phospholipids, 42, 43
photons, 69
photosynthesis
   biotechnology and, 68–72
   chloroplasts and, 65–67
   overview of, 64–65
   reactions of, 68
photosystems, 67
pigments, 66, 72
plants, 43, 50–51, 53
polarity, 13, 42, 43
polymerase chain reaction
   (PCR), 77
polypeptides, 9, 15
polysaccharides, 48, 49
porin, 24
porphyria, 63
porphyrin pathway, 61
porphyrins, 65–66
potassium pumps, 24
preservatives, 49
primary protein structure, 17–19
prisms, 66
progesterone, 46
proline, 11
proteases, 34, 57
proteins
   amino acids and, 12
   digestion and, 56
   functions of, 22–24
   globular or fibrous structure
      of, 22
   overview of, 2, 16–17
   primary structure of, 17–19
   proteomics and, 79
   quaternary structure of, 18, 22
   secondary structure of, 18, 19–20
   tertiary structure of, 18, 20–22
protein sequencing, 19
protein synthesis, 2
proteomes, 79
proteomics, 79
pumps, protein, 24
purines, 25
purity, defined, 10
pyrimidines, 25
pyruvate, 60

Q

quaternary protein structure, 22

R

radioisotope labeling
   experiments, 4
reflection, 69
refraction, 69
replication, 26, 28–29, 36–38
respiration. *See* Cellular respiration
rhodopsin, 24
ribosomes, 73
RNA, 2, 29
RNA polymerase, 36–38

S

saccharides, 48
Sanger, Fredrick, 70
saturated fats, 41
scurvy, 7
secondary protein structure, 18,
   19–20
semi-permeable, defined, 42
sequencing, DNA, 74, 76
serine, 11
serum albumin, 23

sex hormones, 45–46
sickle-cell anemia, 5–6
signal transduction, 5
silicon, 70–71
skiing, wax and, 45
sodium pumps, 24
solar energy cells, 70–72
solubility, vitamins and, 46–47
specificity, enzyme, 34
spectroscopy, 4
Stanley, Wendell M., 70
starches, 2, 49, 50, 56–57
steroids, 36, 44–46, 47
sterols, 44
stomata, 65
storage proteins, 24
structural maintenance, 24, 50
substrates, enzymes and, 31–34
sucrose, 49
sucrose zymase, 62
sugar groups, 24–25, 27
sugars
    carbohydrates and, 2, 48–49, 52
    chloroplasts and, 65
    digestion and, 55
    fermentation and, 52
Sumner, James B., 70
sunlight, 66
sunscreens, 66
symbols chemical, 10
Szent-Györgyi, Albert, 7

T
Taq polymerase, 77
techniques, 4
temperature, enzyme activity
    and, 33
templates, 76, 80
termites, 51
tertiary protein structure, 18,
    20–21, 70
testosterone, 45–46
threonine, 11
thrombin, 24

thylakoid membranes, 65, 67
thymine, 24–27
trachea, 23
transferrin, 24
transfer RNA (tRNA), 30
transport proteins, 24
triglycerides, 40–41
tryptophan, 11
tubulin, 23
tyrosine, 11, 63

U
ultraviolet (UV) radiation, 66
unsaturated fats, 41
uracil, 24–25, 30
urea, 62
urea cycle, 61

V
valine, 11
viruses, 26
vitamins, 7, 46–47

W
water, 12–14, 65
Watson, James, 71
wave, light as, 69
wavelengths, 66–67, 69
waxes, 42–44, 45
Wilkins, Maurice, 71
wine, 52
Wöhler, Friedrich, 62

X
X-ray crystallography, 4, 70,
    79–80
xylem, 65

Y
yeast, 52
yogurt, 59

Z
zymase, 62

ABOUT THE AUTHOR

MONIQUE LABERGE received a Ph.D. in Physical Chemistry from McGill University. Her postdoctoral training was conducted in the Department of Biochemistry and Biophysics at the University of Pennsylvania, where she is now a Senior Research Investigator. Dr. Laberge has taught protein structure and dynamics courses at Semmelweis University, where she was a guest scientist from 2000 to 2005. Her research and publications are in the field of biomolecular simulations focused on the role of dynamics in protein function. Dr. Laberge has previously authored *Cracking the GRE Chemistry*, a compendium of her extensive chemistry tutorials, published by Random House and now in its second edition.